HORNBY
magazine

What's inside...

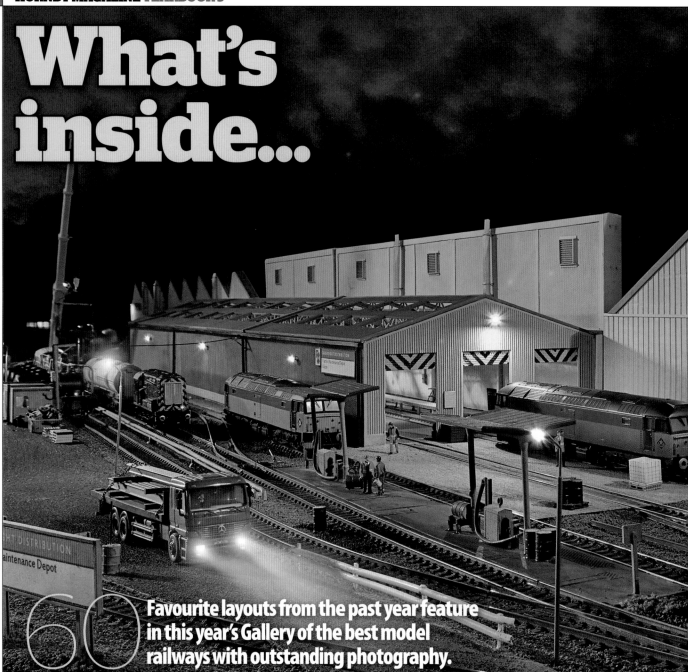

60 Favourite layouts from the past year feature in this year's Gallery of the best model railways with outstanding photography.

48

It might be an American
building, but we've made it British.

Simple detailing can bring life and
atmosphere to models. We show you how.

Hornby Magazine's annual Review of the Year
covers all the highlights from 2015 and 2016.

EDITORIAL
Editor: Mike Wild
Assistant Editor: Mark Chivers
Sub Editor: Andy Roden
Contributors: Evan Green-Hughes, Tim Shackleton,
Paul Chetter, Julia Scarlett and Ian Wild.
Senior designer: Steve Diggle

REGISTERED OFFICE
Units 1-4, Gwash Way Industrial Estate, Ryhall Road,
Stamford, Lincs PE9 1XP

PRINTING
Gomer Press Limited, Llandysul
Ceredigion, South Wales.

ADVERTISING
Advertising: Sarah Jarman
Email: sarah.jarman@keypublishing.com
Tel: 01780 755131 **Fax:** 01780 757261
Advertising Production: Rebecca Duffy
Tel: 01780 755131
Fax: 01780 757261
Email: rebecca.duffy@keypublishing.co.uk

PUBLISHING
Publisher: Adrian Cox
Tel: 01780 755131
Fax: 01780 757261
Email: adrian.cox@keypublishing.com

Executive Chairman: Richard Cox
Managing Director: Adrian Cox
Commercial Director: Ann Saundry
Sales & Marketing Manager: Martin Steele

KEY **Key Publishing Ltd,**
Units 1-4, Gwash Way Industrial Estate
Ryhall Road Stamford, Lincs PE9 1XP

Welcome

Grosvenor Square is *Hornby Magazine's* latest project layout which models a West Midlands located Western Region terminus station.

THE ANTICIPATION of arriving at a station and finding out what is at the head of the train is full of excitement. I remember, probably 20 years ago now, arriving at the East Lancashire Railway for one of its high-profile diesel events. As we walked into the booking hall the distinctive burble of a 'Western' diesel-hydraulic could be heard on the platforms below.

That day – and many other moments with the Western Region 'hydraulics' – have all inspired my interest in this select group of locomotives. I never saw them in service, but I have always believed them to have been a spectacular part of the railway scene.

In part that is what we have set out to create in this year's annual Yearbook project layout – the thrill of arriving at the station ready for a day out. You never know what might be in the platform waiting for departure, but as you walk into the booking hall on our 'OO' gauge layout Grosvenor Square, you can be sure that there will be a whiff of Western Region steam or the rumble of a 'hydraulic' to whet your appetite.

This year we have set our focus on terminus station operation, although there is plenty of other content for you to feast on. The centrepiece of this is our latest project which is the start of what will eventually become a 25ft long 'OO' gauge layout showcasing the full potential of a working railway terminus.

That ideal of operational value has been a key part of the layout build. Digital Command Control, sound and a full live track layout really open up the possibilities and all of the team are eager to get behind the controls and bring Grosvenor Square to life at the Warley National Model Railway Exhibition in November 2016.

The build is just one part of this Yearbook. You can read about railway history and we've put together other projects which can suit any layout from any area of the country, ranging from sound fitting to building construction, platform construction and much more.

We are also looking back on the highlights of 2016 and looking forward to the coming year where our manufacturers are offering some wonderful prospects. The past 12 months have been incredibly busy once again and it is encouraging to see a steady procession of products leaving Hornby's warehouse for sale to its eager customers.

There have been some significant moments during 2016 in model production including Sutton's Locomotive Works' Sulzer Type 2 for detail and sound, Dapol's Black Label Gresley 'A4' for its operational value and potential and, on the opposite end of the scale, Bachmann's delightful Wickham Type 27 trolley which arrived in the final weeks before this book closed for press. We've seen two models of the Adams 'Radial' 4-4-2T arrive in 'OO' plus the first North Eastern Region locomotive in ready-to-run form in the Raven 'Q6' 0-8-0 from Hornby. Oh, and don't forget Locomotion Models' inspired model of the Advanced Passenger Train – Experimental, Revolution Trains' proving of the crowd-funding route in its TEA 100ton tanker for 'N' gauge and all the other models which have made 2016 so interesting.

Our wonderful hobby continues to bring new inspirations and products to the fore and we can't wait to see what 2017 has to offer as more new models arrive and are announced.

Happy modelling! ∎

Mike Wild
Editor, *Hornby Magazine*

TOP 20 OF 2016

Hundreds of products pass through the *Hornby Magazine* editorial office every year. We highlight **20 of the best** which we have tested or worked with in 2016.

Hornby 'Q6' 0-8-0
■ *www.hornby.com* ■ **£139.99** ■ 'OO' gauge

As the first ever ready-to-run North Eastern Railway prototype, Hornby's 'OO' gauge model of the Raven 'Q6' 0-8-0 gets our vote without a shadow of a doubt. Superbly produced with excellent attention to detail and outstanding performance this model deserves popularity.

It was released in June 2016 with three versions making up the first batch covering 3418 in LNER black, 63443 in BR black with early crests and 63429 in BR black with late crests. Subtle detail variations were incorporated into each model while all three employed a flywheel driven motor and an 8-pin DCC socket in the tender.

Models specifically for the North Eastern Region have been highly sought after and this is a big tick off the list.

Zimo MX649 decoder
■ *www.zimo.at*
■ **£98.00**
■ 'N' and 'OO' gauge

The Zimo MX649 sound decoder might not have the most exciting name, but its compact 23mm x 9mm x 4mm profile has opened up a new world of possibilities for installing sound in space-starved locomotives.

In particular this new decoder specification has allowed a wider range of 'N' gauge motive power to be equipped simply and effectively in combination with the manufacturer's impressive 8mm sugar cube speaker.

Its specification includes DCC and analogue modes, four function outputs, 1watt audio for six channels with an 8ohm speaker output, 0.7amp motor rating and all standard Zimo features.

So, if you have a compact locomotive that you want to install sound in with a 6-pin, 8-pin or hard wire connection the MX649 is well worth considering.

Dapol Southern Railway rail built signals

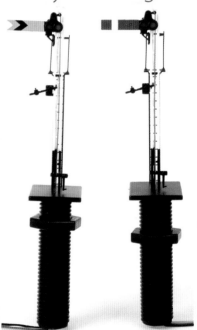

■ *www.dapol.co.uk* ■ **£30.45** ■ 'OO' gauge

Dapol's ready-built signals have filled a gap in the market which many have been calling out for. Here at *Hornby Magazine* we've enjoyed using the BR pattern signals on several layouts and in 2016 the manufacturer released its Southern Railway rail built versions in both stop and distant styles. Executed superbly and simple to install these new signals expand the range available and are soon to be bolstered by Southern Railway lattice post platform signals too.

DCC Concepts Alpha Central
■ *www.dccconcepts.com*
■ **£155.00** ■ All scales

DCC Concepts has a strong reputation for quality control equipment and the Alpha Central unit is a superbly crafted piece. But what does the sleek aluminium box do? Well, in short, this is a bespoke point control handset for use with Digital Command Control.

It can be plugged directly into the NCE system to operate up to 12 points or accessories independently of the other handsets or, through the DCC Concepts adapters, it can be connected to any DCC system to achieve the same.

Introduced in November 2015 it landed on our desk for review in early 2016 and is a fantastic piece of kit. Illuminated touch button LEDs provide the contacts to operate accessories while stainless steel etched numberplates are included for fitting after purchase to identify each button's operation. It is fully programmable in blocks of 12 and multiple Alpha Central units can be used to create a larger control panel.

This is the first out of the box control panel – and it's great!

Dapol Black Label Gresley 'A4'

- www.dapol.co.uk
- £399.95
- 'OO' gauge

Dapol is moving model railway locomotive design forward with its new Black Label Gresley 'A4' 4-6-2 for 'OO' gauge. Designed from the outset to be different from the rest, the Black Label 'A4' offers a powerful locomotive with a die-cast body, fan driven smoke generator, factory installed digital sound, firebox flicker, working lamps and more.

It is being produced in limited quantities for release before the end of 2016 with *Hornby Magazine's* exclusive first review being published in HM114 (December 2016). The model is of the original condition locomotives with availability in LNER garter blue, silver and apple green.

It is the first time that a ready-to-run model has been produced with a factory fitted smoke generator in recent times and takes the level of operation available to the modeller to a new level. Eye catching, enjoyable and superbly finished, the Black Label 'A4' takes locomotive design to a new level – and one we hope to see more of in the future.

Hornby LSWR Maunsell 58ft stock

- www.hornby.com ■ £44.99 each ■ 'OO' gauge

Hornby is well versed in modelling Maunsell carriages and in 2016 it released a new collection of ex-LSWR Maunsell rebuilds in both Southern Railway olive green and BR crimson liveries.

These non-corridor carriages complement the manufacturer's already impressive range of coaching stock well and fill a gap in the market for Southern Region suburban carriages. Each is suitably detailed with the range covering an eight-compartment brake third, six-compartment lavatory brake third, six-compartment lavatory composite and nine-compartment lavatory third.

Gaugemaster wheel cleaner

- www.gaugemaster.com
- £19.95 ■ 'OO' and 'N' gauge

Keeping trains moving means clean wheels and Gaugemaster has released this simple wheel cleaning brush which mounts on the track to take power to make this important process simple. We've been thoroughly impressed by this wheel cleaning device and it now travels to every exhibition with our layouts. It's so good we've even bought one for 'N' gauge too and it keeps our trains moving smoothly with the minimum of fuss.

Oxford Diecast Komatsu excavator

- www.oxforddiecast.co.uk ■ £20.95 ■ 'OO' gauge

Plant vehicles are always distinctive and for the modern layout builder the Komatsu excavator from Oxford Diecast is an absolute must-have in our book. Detailed, striking and featuring a poseable boom and cab this 1:76 scale model will be the perfect starting point for a cameo scene on a post 2000 period model railway.

Lifecolor Liquid Pigments

■ **www.airbrushes.com** ■ **£17.50 (six pack)** ■ **All scales**

An unusual choice considering the other elections for this top 20 feature, but Lifecolor's Liquid Pigments have become an essential part of our painting armoury. Several sets of six have been produced all with potential for model railway application, but here we will focus on the Trains and Tracks set.

These acrylic based paints are designed to be used as washes and after application they can be manipulated with the 'remover' included with each set. This opens up infinite possibilities when it comes to weathering and detailing locomotives, rolling stock, track, buildings and more.

Simple though they may be, the Lifecolor Liquid Pigments are versatile and a new 'must-have' for our workbench.

Redutex brick sheeting

■ **www.redutex.com** ■ **From £6.50 per sheet** ■ **'N' and 'OO' scales**

Redutex is a Spanish company which produces self-adhesive resin based pre-coloured textures covering a wide range of wall, paving and roofing materials across a number of scales.

Its products aren't particularly well known in the UK just yet, but they really should be. We've used the Redutex texture sheets on a number of *Hornby Magazine* projects in 2016 and highly recommend this versatile product range. You can see it on this year's project layout – Grosvenor Square – where we have used it for the platform edging, retaining walls, low relief buildings and more.

It isn't brand new, but the range continues to expand and is well worth investigating.

Graham Farish DCC sound fitted Class 108

■ **www.bachmann.co.uk**
■ **£269.95** ■ **'N' gauge**

Sound has become commonplace in 'OO' and 'O' gauge models, but in 'N' gauge it has been regarded generally as either a novelty with little realism or just plain impossible. But following the launch of Zimo's MX649 decoder series, Bachmann has taken on the challenge to deliver a factory sound fitted model – and this one is no novelty.

The recordings and sound output from the Zimo sugar cube speaker – a combination we are familiar with here at the *Hornby Magazine* office – are nothing short of excellent and, to make it even more enticing, the decoder can recreate gear changes automatically and on demand through intervention from the throttle. It even has the option to set the unit into fourth gear at any point through a function button press and delivers all the rasp and atmosphere of a rattling first generation unit you could want.

Hornby Twin Track Sound Class 67

■ **www.hornby.com** ■ **£169.99** ■ **'OO' gauge**

Hornby's Twin Track Sound (TTS) range of Digital Command Control diesel locomotives is capturing attention – not least because of the budget price of the sound decoders. Though the price may be small, their abilities are excellent with impressive driving control facilities and quality sound output. They are a perfect stepping stone into the world of digital sound and serve to make this exciting part of the market more accessible.

The Class 67 captures the distinctive sound of these high-speed diesel-electric locomotives well and with more than 20 sound functions on board it offers a great deal of operational value too.

Locomotion Models APT-E

- www.locomotionmodels.com
- £225 (DCC ready), £325 (DCC sound fitted)
- 'OO' gauge

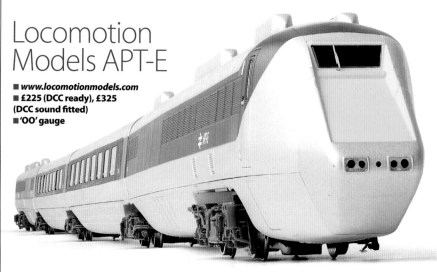

The Advanced Passenger Train – Experimental was an out of the box idea when it was first mooted in the late 1960s – its concept being to develop a train capable of running at 150mph. It only ever ran on test, but the gas turbine powered four-car unit holds a special place in British Railway history.

Enter Canadian manufacturer Rapido Trains and a deal with Locomotion Models to produce a short run limited edition for the National Collection in Miniature series – a product which it delivered in April 2016.

This stunning model – offered as a four-car train pack with the option to buy an additional pair of trailers – met impressive levels of detail inside and out, offers factory fitted sound, a fully working tilt system and more.

Impressive it most certainly is and stocks flew off the shelves through sheer demand making this a sought after limited edition.

Bachmann Blue Pullman version 2.0

- www.bachmann.co.uk
- £599.95
- 'OO' gauge

The Blue Pullman is an icon of luxury rail travel. Bachmann's first model arrived in 2012 to great fanfare while this year it has produced a second version in a special presentation pack.

It uses the same stunning model as the original release, but this time it comes without DCC decoders fitted but with a pack of train crew figures, a copy of a painting of the Pullman, a history of the train, menu and a numbered certificate. The catch? The price is higher than the first version.

Nevertheless, there is no questioning the qualities of the Bachmann Blue Pullman which has become a highly sought after train. This model will undoubtedly go down in history and will become a collector's piece.

Dapol 'N' gauge 'Schools'

- www.dapol.co.uk
- £142.05
- 'N' gauge

The Maunsell 'Schools' 4-4-0 is the latest steam locomotive to be produced for 'N' gauge by Dapol. The 1930 introduced 'Schools' were the most powerful 4-4-0s in Britain at the time and were capable of handling the Southern Railway's heaviest trains.

Dapol's new model has had a long gestation, but the wait was definitely worth it. It has released the 4-4-0 in Southern Railway olive and malachite greens, BR lined black and BR lined green with excellent attention to detail, impressive haulage capability and DCC compatibility.

For the Southern Region modeller this new release couldn't come soon enough and with its arrival we are eagerly awaiting Dapol's air-smoothed and rebuilt Bulleid 'Light Pacifics' which are being developed for 'N' gauge too.

Indexing drive turntable

- www.admturntables.co.uk
- £410.00 ■ 'N' and 'OO' scales

Although not strictly a new product in 2016 we had the opportunity of first hand experience with one of ADM Turntables' indexing drive turntables in the first of our 24hr challenge layouts in the first quarter of the year.

The turntable system is built around the Peco well turntable and is available for both 'OO' and 'N' gauge. ADM's system can be stopped at over 2,000 positions around the turntable's diameter and is available in analogue and digital formats – the latter offering a live bridge which means light and sound can be maintained on locomotives throughout a revolution of the turntable.

Making life even simpler ADM has developed an adapter ring which means that a square section needs to be cut from the baseboard surface (rather than a more difficult circle) and a secondary mount allows the turntable to be lowered out for maintenance or detailing when required.

Sutton's Locomotive Works Class 24

■ *www.sulzertype2.co.uk* ■ **£160 (DCC ready), £260 (DCC sound fitted)** ■ **'OO' gauge**

We have come to expect a certain level of detail and quality for ready-to-run locomotives, but Sutton's Locomotive Works' (SLW) entry to the 'OO' gauge market re-wrote the book on what was possible.

Announced in November 2015, and immediately available, the SLW Class 24 is a cut above the rest offering stunning detail and accuracy and one of the most comprehensive and realistic sound decoder packages we have seen in a mass-produced model.

Operating with a Zimo Plux22 MX645 decoder the sound file created by Paul Chetter is played through a pair of high quality speakers which lift the lid on the potential of digital sound.

Heljan 'O' gauge 'Warship'

■ *www.heljan.dk* ■ **£699.00** ■ **'O' gauge**

The Western Region's 'Warship' diesel-hydraulics were as distinctive in sound as they were in appearance and to be able to own one of these imposing locomotives in 'O' gauge is a great prospect. Heljan delivered a superb version of the Class 42 Swindon-built locomotives in 2016 for 7mm scale with a choice of BR green, BR maroon and BR blue liveries.

We had the opportunity to inspect BR maroon liveried D869 *Zest* – a model which delivered on all levels with smooth running twin motors, separately powered roof fans, directional lighting and a superbly modelled body.

Since release it has been a popular seller and is a perfect partner to Heljan's previous 'O' gauge models of the 'Hymek' and 'Western' hydraulics.

Wickham trolley and trailer

■ *www.bachmann.co.uk*
■ **£79.95**
■ **'OO' gauge**

When Bachmann's Wickham trolley landed in the *Hornby Magazine* office the first thing which struck us about it was its size. This tiny, and beautifully detailed, model is something quite different and shows the strength of the ready-to-run market to support the extraordinary.

Traditionally this kind of rolling stock has been produced as a static item to allow it to be posed alongside the railway, but Bachmann has taken up the challenge to make its Type 27 Wickham fully operational. A motor is contained within the tiny ballast trailer which propels the finely detailed trolley along the track.

This is that something different – an out of the ordinary product which is sure to prove popular.

Bachmann '64XX' 0-6-0PT in 'N'

■ *www.bachmann.co.uk*
■ **£94.95**
■ **'N' gauge**

Small locomotives present great challenges in 'N' gauge and Bachmann rose to the occasion with its delightful model of the GWR '64XX' 0-6-0PT.

The diminutive '64' has been produced in GWR green, BR black and BR lined green. Each is DCC ready with a right angled six-pin socket inside while the running qualities and details are second to none.

Bachmann's coreless motor has worked wonders for its 'N' gauge locomotive range taking performance of its steam models to the highest levels.

The '64XX' is soon to be joined by a Hawksworth autocoach in 'N' gauge too allowing prototypical auto trains to be modelled in the scale.

Introducing GROSVENOR SQUARE

Termini make wonderful railway models and this year the *Hornby Magazine* team has embarked on a new project to create a Western Region theme station set in the Midlands. **MIKE WILD** introduces Grosvenor Square.

A Bachmann Class 43 draws out across the newly laid junction at Grosvenor Square. With seven platforms this layout is sure to entertain.

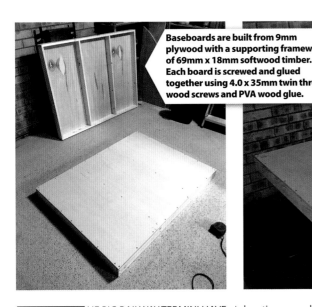

Baseboards are built from 9mm plywood with a supporting framework of 69mm x 18mm softwood timber. Each board is screwed and glued together using 4.0 x 35mm twin thread wood screws and PVA wood glue.

The first phase of the project concentrates on three baseboards making up 12ft of the total 16ft scenic section.

THE BIG RAILWAY TERMINI HAVE been likened to cathedrals. Their grand architecture and the sheer size of the train sheds which cover the passengers and railway staff beneath dominate skylines in major cities.

Finding land close to a city centre was difficult for the railway developers. Prices were high and the physical space needed was often difficult to obtain. In other locations (Crewe and Doncaster spring to mind) the town developed around the railway, but when it came to places like London and Birmingham the opposite was true – the railway had to fit around the city. That is one of the great challenges to layout builders – developing a layout where the railway, our prime interest, plays second fiddle to the rest of the world.

There is a high chance that many will be able to recall a visual in their mind's eye of what the inside of London Paddington station looks like – one of the best known and most stunning pieces of railway terminus design in the world – and it is terminus stations like this where trains meet their journey's end that has inspired us to create this new layout for the *Hornby Magazine* exhibition roster.

Grosvenor Square isn't set in London as there are plenty of other options for a terminus away from the capital. Our choice started out with a desire to create a Western Region themed layout, but we didn't want to pick a clichéd location on the South West coast. Instead we opted for the opposite corner of Western Region operations by choosing a Midlands

location served by the Western Region from the south and, for added variety, on occasion by the Midland Region from the north. The inclusion of two regions makes for interesting operating practices too which we will come on to later on in this Yearbook.

Choosing a style

Terminus stations range in size from single platform quaint country branch lines to giant multiple platform affairs serving hundreds of trains a day. From a modelling point of view the simplest is the branch line – a single platform and a small goods yard can provide ample opportunity for modelling and operation, especially for a home layout, but we wanted to create something on a larger scale which represented a main line terminus capable of handling express locomotives and a variety of train formations.

The initial specification for Grosvenor Square called for at least seven platform faces, automatic uncoupling of locomotives from arriving trains, Digital Command Control (DCC) operation, seven carriage trains and, as an absolute must, an overall roof for over half of the station area combined with an imposing station building.

That list was tough to replicate in the real world, but with pen and paper to hand we set about drawing out ideas to create our version of a Western Region terminus station. Initial thoughts centred around a multi-phase plan which would incorporate the roundhouse scene built for the first 24hr challenge project in HM105 as well as carriage sidings, a main »

TOOLS

Track laying and wiring
» Pencil
» Craft knife
» Track cutters
» Pin hammer
» Pin punch
» Pin vice and 1mm drill bit
» Pliers
» Mini drill
» Cutting disc for mini drill
» Wire strippers
» Soldering iron

Baseboard construction
» Tape measure
» Pencil
» Tri-square
» Handsaw
» Electric screwdriver
» Crosshead screwdriver bit
» Electric drill
» 2mm, 7mm, 9mm drill bits
» G-clamps
» Flat file

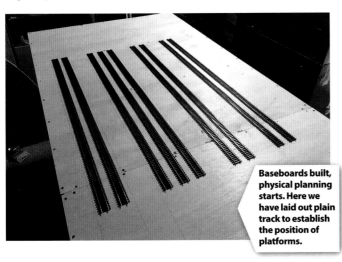

Baseboards built, physical planning starts. Here we have laid out plain track to establish the position of platforms.

Mocking up point formations using suitable locomotives and rolling stock checks the important dimensions – and especially those for the headshunts.

STEP BY STEP / **INSTALLING KADEE PERMANENT MAGNETS**

1 To provide automatic uncoupling using Kadee couplings we opted to install under the track permanent magnets at strategic locations. Holes need to be cut in the baseboard to accept these magnets – this is how we did it…

2

Beginner — Intermediate — Advanced
SKILL LEVEL

Draw around the magnet in the position you want to install it taking care to ensure it is aligned under the centre of the track.

3 Using a 9mm wood drill, drill four holes – one in each corner of the magnet opening.

4 Continue drilling holes with the same drill bit to fill in the gaps between the corner holes, then by angling the drill the holes can be fully connected to allow the centre to drop out.

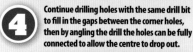

5 With the centre out there is more to do as it is essential to get a snug fit for the magnet into the baseboard.

6 Having cleaned up the faces of the hole and checked for fit, the magnet is pressed into place and glued into the baseboard with contact adhesive.

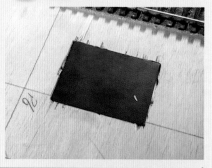

TIP

Using the right type of drill bit for the material you are working with is important. When drilling through wood always use wood specific drill bits as they have sharp points which help to guide the drill through the material accurately.

7

8

The track is then returned over the top of the magnet meaning that once ballasted the magnet below will be totally invisible.

With Kadee couplings fitted to locomotive and carriage the magnets allow automatic uncoupling with the correct sequence of events. Happily, they won't uncouple trains when the couplings are under tension.

line run and a long storage yard at the rear of a 'U' shape layout. That proved to be more of a challenge than we could feasibly handle in the time available so instead we looked towards reusing one of the storage yards from Twelve Trees Junction to create a straight fronted layout which could accommodate the station, a goods warehouse scene and, possibly, a small set of carriage sidings. There is no reason why in future we couldn't come back to the layout and extend it further though. The total scenic length proposed for this plan was 16ft which would increase to 25ft when a 9ft storage yard from Twelve Trees Junction (*Hornby Magazine Yearbook No. 6*) was bolted on too.

For the purpose of this Yearbook, we will be focusing our efforts on the first three of the four baseboards for the scenic section which cover 12ft of the planned total scenic section. For future development the fourth baseboard will feature the inbound junctions as well as a large goods warehouse and sidings capable of handling parcels and van traffic to increase the operational interest available to the team when Grosvenor Square is exhibited.

Starting point

As with all layouts our first port of call after establishing the length of the layout was to work out how wide the boards would be. To accommodate seven platforms and associated carriage sidings at the rear – plus a narrow area of low relief buildings and backdrop – meant we needed to build 3ft wide baseboards. Each would be 4ft long allowing all baseboards to be built to a standard size for the 16ft scenic section. This in turn eases transport and storage with baseboards all conforming to the same dimensions.

The railway would be supported on solid

While we didn't want to emulate the Western Region coastal terminus of Penzance, certain features influenced Grosvenor Square's design including the part length overall roof. On July 9 1953 GWR 'Hall' 6949 *Haberfield Hall* departs Penzance with the 'Cornish Riviera'.
Lewis Coles/Rail Archive Stephenson.

This is the full 16ft length during planning – the nearest baseboard remains to be built.

Gaugemaster 1/16in thick cork has been laid under all of the track formation.

"With the baseboards assembled the task of turning the paper plan into reality was next."

MIKE WILD

top design boards with the surrounding town structures rising above at different levels. The baseboards were assembled using 9mm plywood for the tops supported by a framework of 69mm x 18mm planed softwood timber. This was screwed and glued together using a combination of 4.0 x 35mm twin thread wood screws and PVA wood glue to create solid, strong and rigid baseboards capable of supporting all the railway operations we wanted above. Legs for the layout will be shared with Twelve Trees Junction, which has the same size baseboards, saving a substantial amount of work and cost. DCC Concepts alignment dowels and M6 coach bolts with

wing nuts bring the baseboards together accurately each time the layout is moved.

With the baseboards assembled the task of turning the paper plan into reality was next. Simple as that may seem, there are always modifications to be made and in fact much of the complex pointwork was finally established in physical planning rather than as a paper exercise.

The difficulty we faced was that we wanted the two inbound and two outbound tracks to be linked so that trains coming in or out could access any platform from any route and vice versa. In the end that required four double slips on the approach tracks combined with large

radius points to create 'ladders' which would allow absolute flexibility over arriving and departing trains. Two of these double slips are located on the fourth baseboard which is yet to be built – it will become the focus of future features in the pages of *Hornby Magazine*.

All of the track for Grosvenor Square is taken from the Peco code 75 range and includes nine large radius points, five double slips and six medium radius points. It has been laid on 1/16in thick cork with copper-clad sleepers positioned either side of each baseboard joint and secured to the rails with solder for solid track mounting. This makes dismantling and moving the exhibition layout simple as we know that all the running rails are firmly fixed in position and won't move.

Our choice of copper-clad sleeper material is 1.5mm thick double sided board from C&L Finescale. This is designed for use in construction of handbuilt turnouts and as such has a similar width to the sleepers on Peco's »

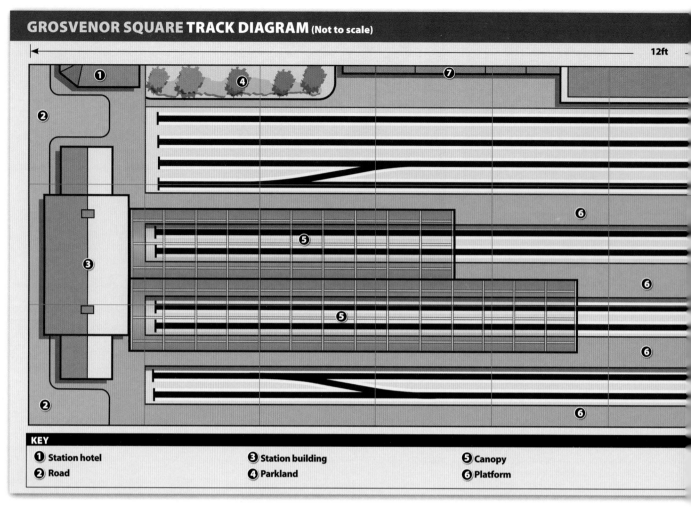

GROSVENOR SQUARE TRACK DIAGRAM (Not to scale)

12ft

KEY

1 Station hotel   **3** Station building   **5** Canopy

2 Road   **4** Parkland   **6** Platform

flexible track. With painting and weathering it is easily disguised making what could be a visually intrusive but essential component of the track formation blend in comfortably.

Magnetic attraction

Automatic uncoupling was an essential item on the specification for the terminus. Because of the desire to have canopies over the station it would be impossible to manually uncouple trains at journeys end so a method had to be sought. Initially there were two options on the table:
1. Retaining tension lock couplings and using uncoupling ramps or thin plastic to lift the

coupling hooks on arrival; or
2. Magnetic uncoupling using the Kadee system of NEM pocket based couplings and permanent magnets.

The first option on paper was the quickest and cheapest, but it would most likely have been unreliable and, particularly on the outer tracks, would have been visually obtrusive too. The big advantage here was cost and time as none of the rolling stock would require modification to operate with uncoupling ramps.

However, whilst a little more involved, we elected to use Kadee couplings and magnets for the layout. They won't be essential on all

trains, but the aim is to achieve hands free uncoupling of all trains in the station area with manual uncoupling of vehicles in the parcels depot to enhance the flexibility of shunting in this area.

There are two main components to the coupling system – permanent magnets which are positioned in holes cut in the baseboard surface and Kadee No. 17-20 NEM style couplings which are a straight replacement for factory fitted tension locks when NEM coupling pockets are provided. There are locomotives without these fittings too and they will require further work to add Kadee magnetic couplings.

Clearance testing for the potential position of the signalbox.

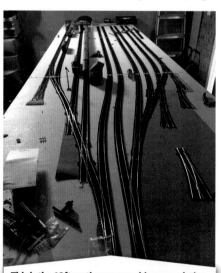

This is the 12ft section approaching completion of track work. On the far left are the DMU carriage sidings and on the far right is the start of the parcels depot.

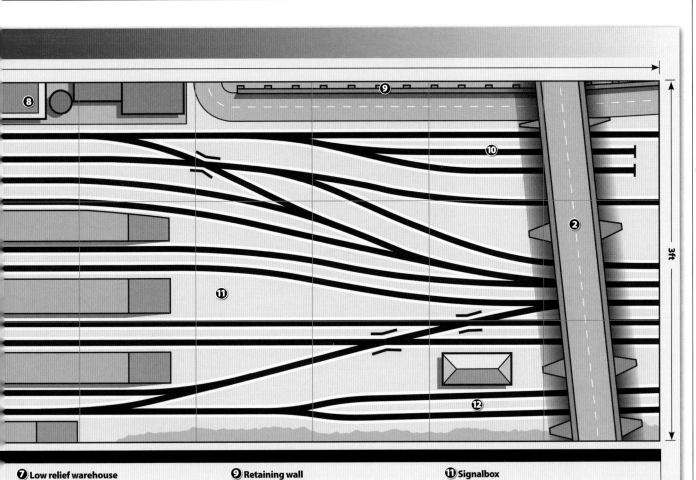

3ft

7 Low relief warehouse
8 Low relief factory
9 Retaining wall
10 Stabling point
11 Signalbox
12 DMU stabling point

Happily, not every vehicle will require a change of couplings. In most cases it will be the locomotive and outer vehicle in each rake of carriages that will require the couplings changing. Some spare vehicles, particularly parcels vans and strengthening carriages, will be fitted with Kadee couplings at both ends and it will take operator knowledge initially to learn how rakes are formed and how they can be operated on the layout.

The step by step guide shows how we installed the permanent magnets and you can see more of the system in action at *www.hornbymagazine.com*

Digital approach

There was only one choice when it came to control of Grosvenor Square and that was DCC. The reasons were simple: reduction in complex wiring and, perhaps more importantly for us, much of the locomotive roster required for the layout had already been sound fitted for operation on our previous Western Region layout St Stephens Road (*Hornby Magazine Yearbook No. 4*). Naturally there will be additions, as St Stephens only needed small and medium sized locomotives so we expect to be adding 'Grange', 'Castle' and 'King' 4-6-0s to the fleet plus a number 'Western' diesel-

hydraulics as a minimum.

For a layout like this terminus digital control offers a great deal of flexibility, especially when it comes to replicating real railway operations. For example, an arriving train can have its locomotive uncoupled using the Kadee permanent magnets before the stock is removed either by the station pilot or by a new train engine. As the departing train advances along the platform, the arriving engine can follow the stock up the platform under independent control before halting at the signal. This is just one example of how digital will benefit this layout.

Checking train lengths is a good opportunity to 'play' with trains. At this point the layout was still unpowered.

Sleepers were cut away from the track either side of each baseboard joint to make way for copperclad sleepers. The latter will secure the track ends at the baseboard joints.

C&L Finescale copper clad strip was used for the securing sleepers. Supplied in lengths it was batch cut to length, drilled for track pins and finally the copper surface (on both sides) cut through to prevent short circuits.

To ensure the full flexibility of digital layout control can be realised, the whole layout has been set up to be wired live – by which we mean that every single section of track has power all the time so that sound and light functions on locomotives and carriages remain in operation at all times. To do this has meant installing insulated rail joiners at strategic positions and a number of extra power feeds to the rails to ensure everything works as it should.

To wire the layout 7/0.2 multi-core equipment wire has been used for the short distance track feeds while 28/0.2 multi-core figure of eight wire has been used to create the long-distance power bus cable which runs the length of the layout. This has been tapped at each baseboard joint to create connections for the track feeds with track power accessories also being connected to the same bus. Point accessory decoder feeds will be taken from a second power bus dedicated to the purpose of operating points and we intend that this will in turn be connected to Hornby's RailMaster computer software for ease of point operation. A computer will be set up behind the layout with a mimic diagram of the full layout on display with

Track feeds were provided by using 7/0.2 multi-core wire. Each was soldered in place and cut, over length, before being fed through 2mm holes either side of the track.

Underneath plug-in terminal blocks provide power connections between the baseboards for the power bus. Power bus wiring is 28/0.2 multi-core figure of eight cable.

the Elite or eLink control unit providing power to the points. Train control will be handled entirely separately by the Gaugemaster Prodigy Advance system.

One of the challenges to overcome with digital control was electrical operation of the double slips. Happily, while the challenge may have been complex the solution was simple – a dual frog juicer from American model railway electronics specialist Tam Valley Depot. We had already had good experience of using the same manufacturer's Hex Frog Juicers (the same type of device but with more outputs) on the live frog diamond crossings on both Twelve Trees Junction and Barrenthorpe, so we knew we were onto a good product. Installation and setup is incredibly simple – connect the two frog wires from the live frog double slip to the frog terminals on the dual frog juicer board and the DCC track feed to the other terminals then turn the power on. It's that easy! The device does all the complex tasks of recognising the polarity required at each frog as a train passes over the double slip meaning that operators only have to

WHAT WE USED	
Product	**Cat No.**
9mm plywood	
69mm x 18mm planed softwood	
PVA wood glue	
4.0 x 35mm twin thread wood screws	
M6 coach bolts	
M6 30mm diameter washers	
M6 wing nuts	
Peco code 75 flexible track	SL-100F
Peco code 75 large radius left points	SL-E189
Peco code 75 large radius right points	SL-E188
Peco code 75 double slips	SL-E190
Peco code 75 medium radius left points	SL-E196
Peco code 75 medium radius right points	SL-E195
Peco code 75 rail joiners	SL-110
Peco code 75 insulated rail joiners	SL-111
Peco track pins	ST-280
Gaugemaster 1/16in cork sheet	GM130
C&L Finescale copper-clad sleeper strips	4ZC101B
Kadee permanent under-the-track uncoupling magnet	308KADEE
Tamiya 10mm masking tape	87034
Tam Valley Dual Frog Juicer	DFJ003U
Humbrol brown spray paint	No. 29

worry about setting the point blades in the right direction for smooth passage of trains.

Rapid progress

By now Grosvenor Square had reached the point of becoming a fully operational layout quickly. It was thoroughly tested both electrically and physically with trials with the Kadee magnets being particularly important at this stage prior to any scenic work commencing.

With testing complete one final job was required before we could start the next phase of work and that was weathering of the track. This task was handled quickly and effectively with three cans of Humbrol No. 29 brown spray paint. The point blades were all masked first with Tamiya 10mm masking tape prior to colouring of the track. Once the paint was fully dry the rail heads were cleaned and the layout tested one more time.

The layout was now ready for the next phase

Development of the final plan involved much physical planning to ensure that point work and operational lengths were correct for the type of trains we would run. This type of planning is essential for a successful terminus layout.

To operate the frogs on the double slips Tam Valley Depot Dual Frog Juicers were installed. These take power from the main power bus circuit and are then connected to the frog wires from the slip. Once installed they take care of polarity change on these points automatically.

of development – building the most substantial feature of the terminus, its platforms. Turn to page 42 to read the next instalment on Grosvenor Square's development. ∎

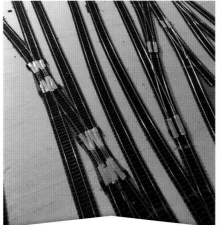

With the wiring and track laying complete next is weathering of the formation. The point blades were all masked first with Tamiya 10mm masking tape.

Humbrol No 29 brown acrylic was then sprayed over the whole track formation to give it a base colour. Rigorous cleaning followed!

Bringing life
to steam locomotives

While steam locomotives acquired their own specific coat and colours of workstaining depending on the traffic they hauled, specific details can make the difference for any engine. **MIKE WILD** picks up a new generation Hornby 'OO' gauge 'King' to show how it can be done.

THE COLLETT 'KING' 4-6-0s were the pride of the Great Western Railway's (GWR) locomotive fleet. Introduced in 1927, in total 31 were built at Swindon Works. The fleet remained in service through the existence of the GWR and went on to serve BR following nationalisation in 1948.

Throughout their career the 'Kings' were used to haul the GWR's heaviest express workings and they continued to do so under BR until the arrival of the diesel-hydraulics in the late 1950s. Ultimately the last of the 'Kings' were withdrawn in 1962 following delivery of the more powerful 'Western' diesels.

Towards the end of their careers the external appearance of the 'Kings' became less well cared for than in their early days, although not in the same way as some of the heavy freight locomotives. However, with staff availability for cleaning being reduced in the final years of steam, oil and soot staining became common.

To boost the locomotive fleet for Grosvenor Square, we wanted to introduce a suitably weathered 'King' to the roster. Hornby introduced its new generation model in 2015 and we had access to a model of 6029 *King Edward VIII* which was duly placed on the painting table to start the detailing process.

All of the colours used on this project are from the Lifecolor acrylic range including one of its recently introduced Liquid Pigments – Smoke. In addition, we used Burned Black, Worn Black, Frame Dirt and – a personal favourite – Dirty Grease Effect. All of these colours complement each other well with none standing out too much over any other.

Completing the 'look' for 6029 are a handful of readily available detailing items. Lamps are from Springside and placed in the express headcode position, the crew is from Master Piece Figures while the fire irons are an etched fret supplied by Kernow Model Rail Centre. One last touch is a load of crushed coal with the distinctive 'shine' of Welsh steam coal.

This 'King' is now ready to enter service with just one addition left to make – a sound decoder to make it sound just as good as it looks. ∎

WHAT WE USED		
Product	**Manufacturer**	**Cat No.**
Burned Black	Lifecolor	UA736
Worn Black	Lifecolor	UA734
Frame Dirt	Lifecolor	UA719
Smoke Liquid Pigment	Lifecolor	LPW21
Dirty Grease Effect	Lifecolor	UA262
GWR pattern lamps	Springside	DA1
Crew	Master Piece Figures	n/a
Fire irons	Kernow Model Rail Centre	K9001

Left inset: **Showing the kind of appearance we have aimed for with the model of 6029, 'King' 6015 *King Richard III* stands at London Paddington with 1M18 for Birmingham on June 23 1962. The locomotive would soon be withdrawn along with the rest of the class.** R A Whitfield/Railphotoprints.co.uk.

Below: **6029 basks in the morning light on the shed turntable as it is prepared for the start of another day. The weathering is a combination of airbrush and hand worked colours, but the details that finish it off are the lamps, crew and coal load.**

STEP BY STEP WEATHERING AND DETAILING A HORNBY 'KING' 4-6-0

1 The starting point: a pristine Hornby 6029 *King Edward VIII*, a Sparmax compressor and Iwata Eclipse airbrush, a painting turntable, a sheet of scrap card and a handful of paint colours.

2

A simple step, but one which is worthwhile, is removing the plastic coal load before starting. This allows weathering of the coal space. We also added the factory supplied detailing pack to the locomotive including brake pipes, brake rigging and cylinder drain cocks.

3

The first step is to soften the colour of the underframe area. You can barely see it here, but a softly airbrushed coat of Burned Black (UA736) is enough to start toning down the factory fresh finish.

4 The wheels, motion and front bogies are all touched up by the Burned Black together with the cab roof.

'King' 6029 *King Edward VIII* leads a rake of Hornby Hawksworth corridor stock – the carriages being weathered with similar colours including Frame Dirt and Roof Dirt from Lifecolor's Rail Weathering set.

Intermediate
Beginner / Advanced
SKILL LEVEL

5

Using the Liquid Pigments Smoke colour (LPW21) we can start adding tone to the boiler cab and tender side. The Smoke colour is washed onto the body and then the Remover liquid supplied in the Liquid Pigment sets is brushed on to start working the colour back.

6 Using a little of the Smoke colour at a time and working it with the Remover builds up neat streaks and soot marks over the boiler and firebox.

7 To further enhance the running gear, Frame Dirt (UA719) is airbrushed lightly over the Burned Black base colours. The Smoke wash is still drying on the boiler at this point.

8 Moving to the tender, the coal space is given a blow over with Frame Dirt (UA719) let down with Lifecolor acrylic thinners. We only need a subtle coat here as a coal load will be added on top.

STEP BY STEP **WEATHERING AND DETAILING A HORNBY 'KING' 4-6-0**

9

10 To adjust the colour of the smokebox – an area which was subjected to intense heat – Worn Black (UA734) has been airbrushed on using a business card as a mask to keep the colour off the green boiler.

Dirty Grease Effect (UA262) is picked up next to add a sheen in the right areas. Everything which moved on a steam locomotive would have oil on it and we have picked out the axleboxes as well as the lubricator pipes, buffer heads and motion with this colour.

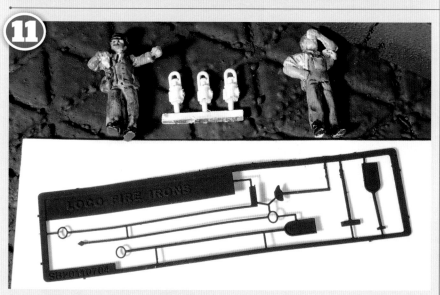

11

Now the details – a Master Piece Figures crew, Springside lamps and a set of fire irons from Kernow Model Rail Centre.

12

The lamps go on first. A spot of superglue is dropped onto a business card so that tweezers can be used to pick up a lamp, dip it in the glue dot and position it on the front footplate.

13

The crew is fixed in the same way. Applying superglue via a business card keeps control of the amount which is used, avoiding unsightly glue marks on the final model.

14

USEFUL CONTACTS	
Lifecolor	www.airbrushes.com
Kernow Model Rail Centre	www.kernowmodelrailcentre.com
Master Piece Figures	01428 727341

15 The finishing touch is a load of crushed coal in the tender. This has been applied over neat PVA, and diluted PVA will be added over the top once the base layer is dry. All that is left to do is clean up the black smears on the tender side.

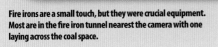

Fire irons are a small touch, but they were crucial equipment. Most are in the fire iron tunnel nearest the camera with one laying across the coal space.

16 A 'King' ready for service on Grosvenor Square – it just needs a sound decoder installing in the tender to finish it off properly.

Terminus *inspiration*

Terminus stations come in all shapes and sizes. **MIKE WILD** rounds up a selection of inspirational layouts which show that variety is the spice of life.

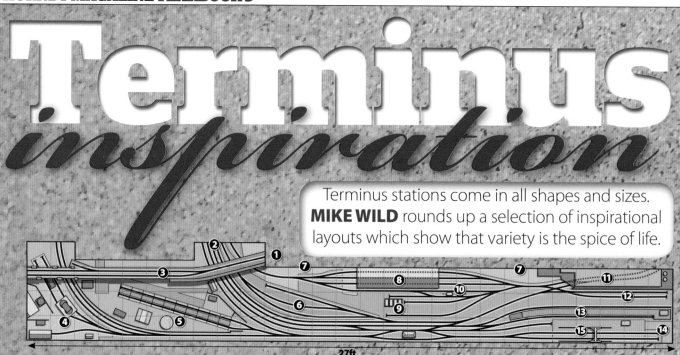

27ft

Oulton TMD

A terminus doesn't have to be the only feature of a model railway and Allan Cromarty's Oulton TMD demonstrates that perfectly. The terminus is just one third of the entire layout which includes a busy Motive Power Depot, industrial sidings and a through line to a steelworks.

The terminus allows passenger operations to mix in between a ready flow of freight traffic on this busy Digital Command Control (DCC) exhibition layout. The terminus allows for locomotive-hauled and multiple unit formations to arrive and depart and, through DCC, multiple trains can be stacked in the same line as shown by the Class 128 and Class 153 Diesel Multiple Units here.

The actual terminus here only offers two platform faces, but, in and amongst all the other activity which is possible on this layout, that is ample.

● **Oulton TMD featured in HM107.**

KEY			
❶	Operating area	❽	Oulton TMD
❷	To storage yard	❾	Fuel storage
❸	Disused railway	❿	Refuelling point
❹	Cement works	⓫	Steel depot
❺	Oil terminal	⓬	Stabling sidings
❻	Ballast yard	⓭	Oulton station
❼	Low relief factories	⓮	Car park
		⓯	Transfer yard

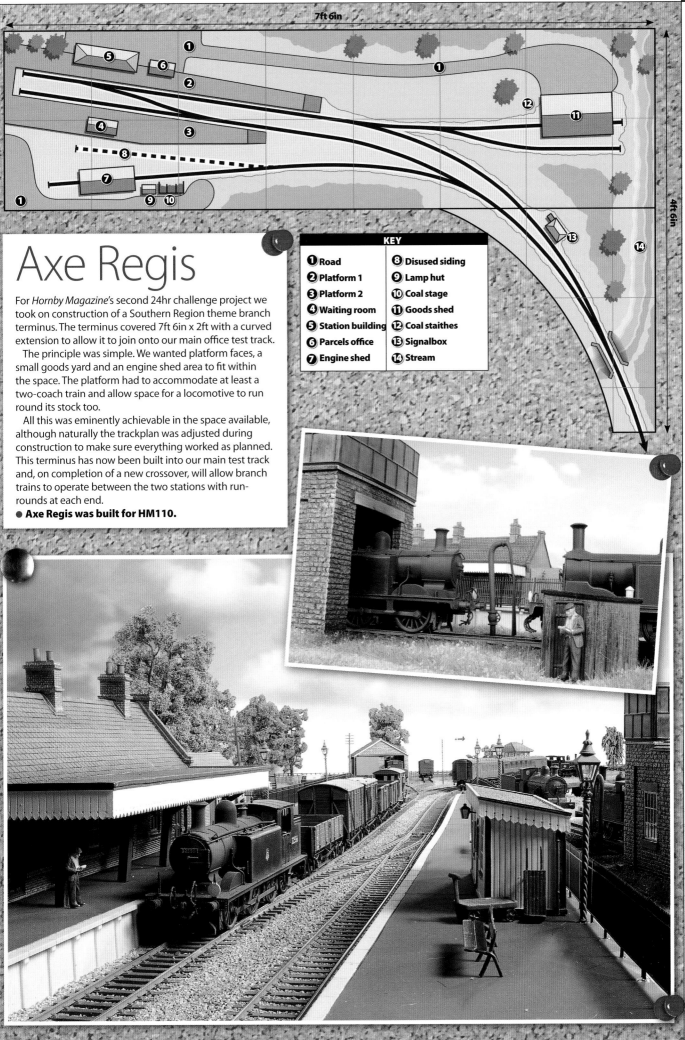

7ft 6in

4ft 6in

KEY

❶ Road	❽ Disused siding
❷ Platform 1	❾ Lamp hut
❸ Platform 2	❿ Coal stage
❹ Waiting room	⓫ Goods shed
❺ Station building	⓬ Coal staithes
❻ Parcels office	⓭ Signalbox
❼ Engine shed	⓮ Stream

Axe Regis

For *Hornby Magazine*'s second 24hr challenge project we took on construction of a Southern Region theme branch terminus. The terminus covered 7ft 6in x 2ft with a curved extension to allow it to join onto our main office test track.

The principle was simple. We wanted platform faces, a small goods yard and an engine shed area to fit within the space. The platform had to accommodate at least a two-coach train and allow space for a locomotive to run round its stock too.

All this was eminently achievable in the space available, although naturally the trackplan was adjusted during construction to make sure everything worked as planned. This terminus has now been built into our main test track and, on completion of a new crossover, will allow branch trains to operate between the two stations with run-rounds at each end.

● **Axe Regis was built for HM110.**

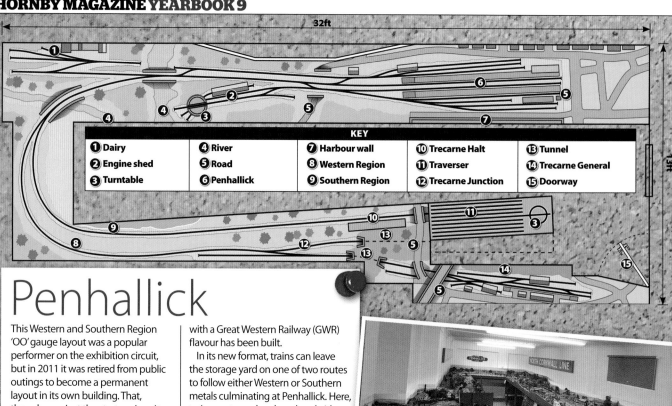

KEY				
1 Dairy	**4** River	**7** Harbour wall	**10** Trecarne Halt	**13** Tunnel
2 Engine shed	**5** Road	**8** Western Region	**11** Traverser	**14** Trecarne General
3 Turntable	**6** Penhallick	**9** Southern Region	**12** Trecarne Junction	**15** Doorway

Penhallick

This Western and Southern Region 'OO' gauge layout was a popular performer on the exhibition circuit, but in 2011 it was retired from public outings to become a permanent layout in its own building. That, though, was just the start as since its retirement it has been developed to include not just one but two termini.

The main station is the original Southern Region location at Penhallick which will be familiar to thousands of exhibition visitors. However, having turned the layout into a 'U' shape and made changes to the junction with the Western Region, a new terminus with a Great Western Railway (GWR) flavour has been built.

In its new format, trains can leave the storage yard on one of two routes to follow either Western or Southern metals culminating at Penhallick. Here, trains are turned and can head either back to the storage yard and the rest of the railway network or take the new route to the Western Region terminus.

It has turned this popular layout into its own mini railway system where each train has a purpose and destination.

● **The revised version of Penhallick featured in HM101.**

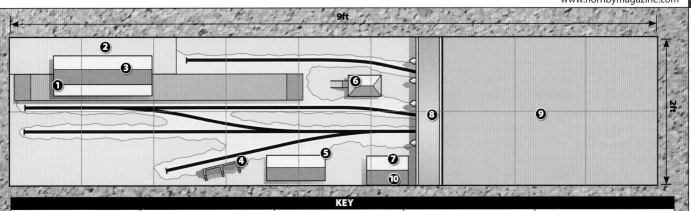

KEY					
❶ Platform	❸ Station building	❺ Garage	❼ Store shed	❾ Traverser fiddle yard
❷ Station forecourt	❹ Coal staithes	❻ Signalbox	❽ Road bridge	❿ Point control

Trebudoc

Andy Peters is a prolific layout builder with a large number of micro layouts under his belt. Trebudoc, which is now in new hands, showed the potential for a compact 'O' gauge branch line terminus scene.

In the limiting 6ft x 2ft footprint of the scenic area, Andy has cleverly included two approach tracks, a station with a bay platform, run-round facilities and a coal yard too – not bad at all for 7mm:1ft scale.

The benefit of all this is that small trains suit branch line locations like this so single coach autotrains and short goods workings are generally the order of the day.

● **Trebudoc featured in HM96.**

47½ft

13ft

STORAGE YARD

KEY					
❶ Houses/shops	❹ Signalbox	❼ Loading dock	❿ Viaduct	⓭ Motive Power Depot	⓰ Coal stage
❷ Road	❺ Station building	❽ Goods yard	⓫ River	⓮ Factory	⓱ Goods shed
❸ Platform	❻ Engine shed	❾ Terrace houses	⓬ Turntable	⓯ Water tower	⓲ Stream

Charnwood Forest Branch

The Soar Valley Model Railway Club's most recent layout is this stunning 'O' gauge model. Measuring 48ft x 13ft, it features a long single track branch line, a passing station and a busy terminus modelled on that at Loughborough Derby Road.

The terminus station area includes a busy motive power depot with a turntable, a goods yard, passing loops and an intensively used single platform station. A run-round loop is in the plan too together with ample opportunity for stock storage and movement.

The complete layout sets out to replicate the majority of a branch line and with the combination of 'main line' running, passing station and terminus it does this very well.

● **The Charnwood Forest Branch featured in HM99 and HM100.**

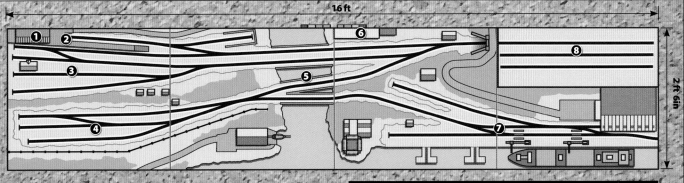

KEY	
❶ Station building	❺ River bridges
❷ Platform	❻ Warehouse
❸ Goods yard	❼ Clay docks
❹ China clay sidings	❽ Storage yard

Porth Eithin

Think of Great Western branch lines and chances are you think of tiny stations with minimal appointment, but Peter Midwinter's Porth Eithin provides a different view with split level operations with passenger and goods on the upper and china clay traffic on the lower. The two are connected and make for an enthralling operational layout.

This 16ft long layout features a trio of river bridges at its centre with the 'main line' crossing a double track bridge to the rear, a descending line on a second bridge to link to the china clay exchange sidings and a third joining the dock to the exchange sidings.

The actual terminus area is quite small consisting of a main platform and bay platform plus a compact goods yard, cattle dock and single road engine shed.

All joined together, this terminus design shows just how different a scheme can be.

● **Porth Eithin is to feature in HM115.**

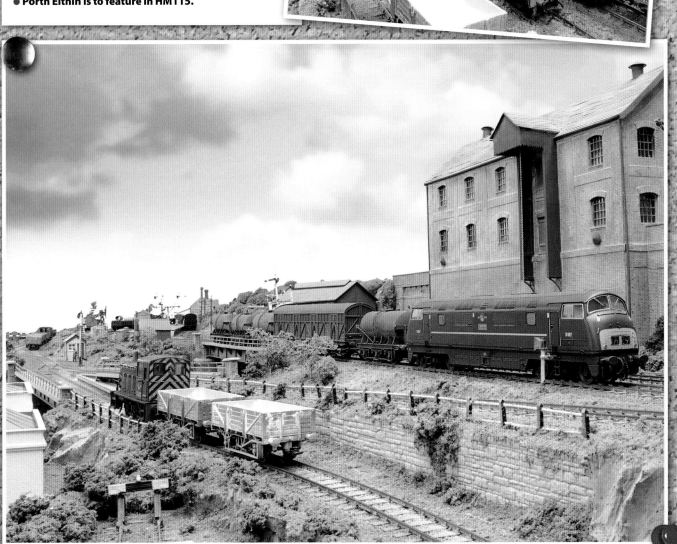

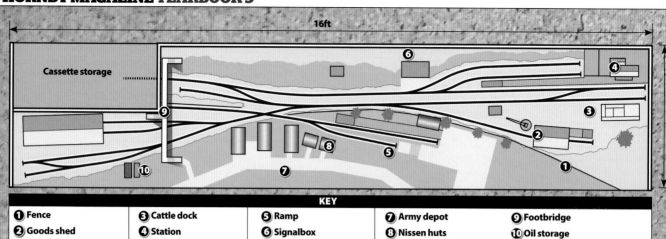

16ft

2ft

Cassette storage

KEY				
① Fence	③ Cattle dock	⑤ Ramp	⑦ Army depot	⑨ Footbridge
② Goods shed	④ Station	⑥ Signalbox	⑧ Nissen huts	⑩ Oil storage

Bigbury

Creating a reason for a railway line is just as important as joining the right track components together. The City of Canterbury Model Railway Society used the combination of a Southern Region branch line terminus and a Ministry of Defence site to create this model called Bigbury.

At 16ft x 2ft it fits a lot into its footprint and offers the opportunity to employ two operators at all times when on show at exhibitions – one for the BR operated route and another to take control of the MoD complex.

Trains are exchanged between the two zones too, increasing operational potential and creating further reasons for the existence of this sleepy country byway.

● **Bigbury featured in HM99.**

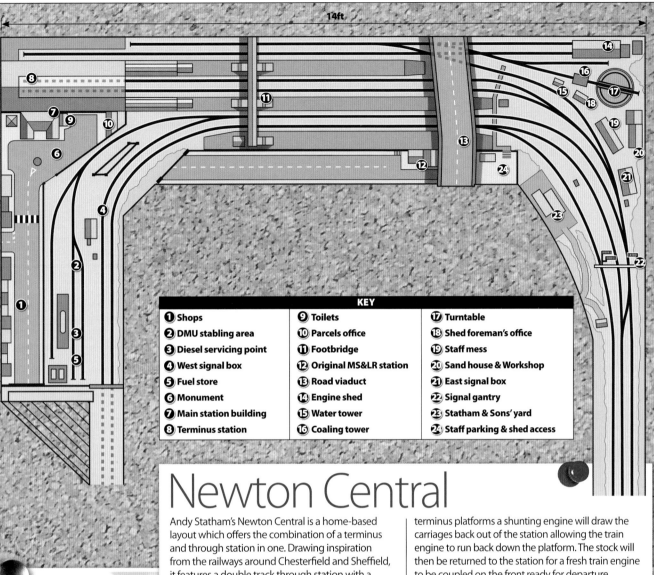

KEY		
❶ Shops	❾ Toilets	⑰ Turntable
❷ DMU stabling area	❿ Parcels office	⑱ Shed foreman's office
❸ Diesel servicing point	⑪ Footbridge	⑲ Staff mess
❹ West signal box	⑫ Original MS&LR station	⑳ Sand house & Workshop
❺ Fuel store	⑬ Road viaduct	㉑ East signal box
❻ Monument	⑭ Engine shed	㉒ Signal gantry
❼ Main station building	⑮ Water tower	㉓ Statham & Sons' yard
❽ Terminus station	⑯ Coaling tower	㉔ Staff parking & shed access

Newton Central

Andy Statham's Newton Central is a home-based layout which offers the combination of a terminus and through station in one. Drawing inspiration from the railways around Chesterfield and Sheffield, it features a double track through station with a terminus to the rear which has an overall roof and a further three platform faces.

The platforms are long enough to accommodate up to six-coach trains and require a shunt release procedure to allow the arriving locomotive to move back to the shed. This means that on arrival in the terminus platforms a shunting engine will draw the carriages back out of the station allowing the train engine to run back down the platform. The stock will then be returned to the station for a fresh train engine to be coupled on the front ready for departure.

To build the overall roof Andy used laser cut parts made specially for him by York Model Making and combined them with a range of readily available card kits for the buildings and retaining walls which surround the railway.

● **Newton Central featured in HM108.**

Terminus

Throughout the railway age the terminus has been an important part of the operational scene

T HE ESTABLISHMENT of the first railways in the early 19th century created new problems that previous transport operators had never had to tackle before. The stagecoaches that ran on the turnpike roads picked up and set down passengers from convenient market squares or more usually from outside public houses and inns. At the end of their journey the coaches were taken to a convenient building where they were put away for the night while the horses were taken to a nearby stable where they could be fed and watered.

When the Stockton & Darlington Railway opened in 1825 passengers were very much a secondary consideration compared with goods traffic. The line had been built to bring coal from the coalfields near Bishop Auckland to the wharves around Stockton where it could be transhipped into boats for onward travel. What stations that existed were quite small and functioned much as had the inns and market squares of the stagecoach age while the line's limits were far beyond the stretch on which passengers usually travelled.

Five years later when George Stephenson was drawing up the plans for the Liverpool & Manchester Railway it was realised that this predominantly passenger line would require something better for its passengers than the occasional use of a room at the inn, and consequently the scheme included provision for a number of proper passenger stations, including one at each end that would accommodate the point at which the line came to a dead end. The idea of the terminus had been born.

After much wrangling between those involved it was decided that the site of Manchester's first terminus station was to be located on land occupied by the dye works of Rothwell and Harrison which was adjacent to Liverpool Road. In choosing the site the promoters of the railway met many of the problems that were to affect builders of later and much larger terminus

London Paddington's grand station its perhaps amongst the most recognisable of all the London termini. Pioneer GWR 'Castle' 4-6-0 4073 *Caerphilly Castle* simmers on arrival with the 8.15am Saturdays only from Abertillery on March 27 1950. A pilot engine will draw up to the rear of the train to remove the passenger stock and release the 'Castle' for servicing. Brian Stephenson

operation

nd one that has brought with it special requirements, as **EVAN GREEN-HUGHES** describes.

stations. Local residents usually did not want a railway, landowners were unwilling to sell and the ideal site for a station was usually too near the centre of the city or town where land was at a premium.

Consequently the station site was away from the city centre. Liverpool was served by Crown Street station, at that time some distance from both the city centre and the docks but in a part of the city where it was possible to acquire sufficient land. Both locations gave the Liverpool & Manchester unique problems that had not been faced before, the primary one being that provision had to be made for a locomotive hauling its carriages to be turned to face the other

way while at the same time being coaled and watered.

In these early days passenger numbers were not particularly high. For some time bookings had to be made 24 hours in advance using the ticket and counterfoil system that was also prevalent on the stagecoaches. This caused passengers some inconvenience as they had to make two trips to the station and consequently a ticket office was opened in the city centre at which bookings could be made.

Only one passenger platform was provided at first at each end of the line and therefore all trains would arrive and depart from the same place. At Liverpool there was a fine overall roof that also

enclosed the two adjoining tracks and which doubled up as a carriage shed each night when the railway had closed down while Manchester managed with an elaborate awning. There were few trains each day and that enabled a fairly relaxed form of working to be introduced in which the locomotive was uncoupled and then driven forwards to a place where it could be turned, a move that was accomplished by the use of a turntable, a device that was already very common on colliery tramways, particularly in the narrow confines of the pithead or even underground where space was at a premium. Due to the relatively small size of the locomotives involved muscle power was sufficient to turn them, after »

which they would be coaled and watered and then re-attached at the opposite end of the same train that they had brought in. At this time it was not common practice for railway locomotives to be run backwards with a train in tow.

This proved satisfactory as long as there was a relatively leisurely timetable with large gaps between trains but was only suitable for locations where there was sufficient room for a length of track beyond the platform onto which the locomotive could be moved for servicing.

Railwaymania

Within a few years these early railways led to a flurry of similar schemes and it was not long before the railway system was knocking on the doors of the nation's capital. However, while the trade brought in by the railway was welcome, little enthusiasm was exhibited for railways inside the capital city itself and consequently lines approaching from the north all came to a halt along the Euston Road.

These terminus stations were initially operated as larger versions of those that already existed with more arrivals and departures, but with trains and locomotives handled in much the same way. However, such longwinded methods soon became impractical particularly as longer platforms were required to serve extended trains and these soon took up the generous amount of space that had originally been allocated at the city end to allow the release of the engine.

An early change was to move the facilities for turning the engines from the interior of the station itself to a location outside, and soon to a purpose-built locomotive depot nearby. The provision of a point just forward of where the train came to a halt allowed the locomotive to be drawn forward from its train and then set

A turning facility was required for steam locomotives at each terminus. In some cases this would be a large depot, where as in others a turntable was provided close to the station. Stanier 'Black Five' 4-6-0 45171 is about to be turned at Edinburgh Princes Street station on August 28 1965. Brian Stephenson.

back on an adjoining track so that it could move onto the servicing facilities. Meanwhile, the train could have a fresh locomotive attached to it and be available for service rather more quickly than previously had been the case.

The railway 'cathedrals'

As the Victorian era drew on the demand for railway travel grew out of all proportion. Stations such as London St Pancras and Kings Cross came under increasing pressure and were expected to cope with far more traffic than they had ever been designed for. Given this situation, the provision of separate tracks to allow locomotives to be released came to be regarded

as something of a luxury and additional platforms were constructed instead. Early stations such as Manchester Liverpool Road and Liverpool Crown Street were too small to cope with the expansion and were soon replaced by much larger installations, and many became goods depots instead.

In some instances, there was not even a locomotive presence in the terminus station. The Liverpool & Manchester's extension into Liverpool itself, which was achieved by cutting a tunnel from Edge Hill, was too steep for early locomotives and so passenger coaches travelled down the slope under gravity and were brought to a halt in the platform by a brakesman. The »

Steam era trainsheds were magnets for dirt and grime, not least because of the exhausts of departing locomotives. On May 14 1956 Reid 'D3' 4-4-0 62426 departs from Edinburgh Princes Street with the 5.22pm for Stirling. W.J. Verden Anderson/Rail Archive Stephenson.

Boasting 14 platforms, Blackpool Central holds the title as the largest station to be closed on the British Railway network. It opened in 1878, was expanded to 14 platforms in 1901 and subsequentely closed in 1964. In this August 1947 view, taken from Blackpool Tower, the impressive size of the coastal terminus and its proximity to the town are clear to see. Much of the land occupied by the station is now either parking or main entry road to the popular location. Stan Garth/Rail Archive Stephenson.

return journey was accomplished by means of a rope which was attached to the carriages with locomotive haulage re-commencing at the summit at Edge Hill.

When Glasgow Queen Street station was opened in 1842 incoming trains were lowered down the 1-in-42 Cowlairs Incline into the station by rope with the locomotive following. The return journey was made with the locomotive on the front of the train but with rope haulage being used to assist, a procedure that was to continue until 1909.

During this period there were a number of terminus stations built in smaller towns, a particularly good example being that at Bath Green Park. Built in 1870 it served the Midland line and later the Somerset & Dorset Joint Railway. Like that built at Inverness in 1855 this was a relatively small terminus but it was one which served as a place where trains would reverse direction to access an ongoing route, as well as reaching the end of their journey. Such arrangements required incoming trains to quickly have another engine attached to the rear, ready

The large termini had grand buildings and imposing trainshed structures. This is the exterior of King's Cross station in March 1967. Colling Turner/ Rail Archive Stephenson.

Even with the advent of diesel traction pilot locomotives were still required to release train engines. 'Deltic' D9001 *St Paddy* and Brush Type 4 D1505 stand at the bufferstops at London King's Cross on arrival with expresses from Newcastle and Leeds respectively on October 5 1963. Brian Stephenson.

to move off again within a few minutes.

A third type of terminus also began to spring up in small towns and villages, with many of these situated at the head of an idyllic branch line that would perhaps only see a handful of trains every day. Workings here were necessarily much more relaxed than at the major sites but still demanded precision and dedication from those who worked them.

By the start of the 20th century the layout of terminus stations was pretty much fixed and those in major cities bore many similarities to each other. There was generally an array of platforms, each fed by an individual track and with many retaining the facility for locomotives to be uncoupled and to run round the stock. Facilities for locomotives had become larger and were usually situated away from the station area. Specialist carriage sidings had also been developed and due to the amount of land that these required were often some distance from the main station.

The exterior of Southampton Terminus station on July 1, 1958. John P. Wilson/Rail Archive Stephenson.

Pilot operations

In the steam era the way the terminus was worked would to a large extent depend on what sort of traffic was handled. Expresses would arrive at one or other of the more prestigious platforms where the locomotive would draw up to the buffer stops and where it would be immediately uncoupled. In the Victorian and Edwardian era it was usual then for a pilot engine – a locomotive selected purely for the movement of passenger and parcels stock in and around the station area - to be coupled onto the other end and after a short time this would be used to draw off the stock and to take it to the carriage sidings where it would be cleaned and serviced ready for its next duty, which may only be in a few hours time.

The locomotive that had brought in the train would follow the empty coaching stock down the platform, in many cases with both trains being on the move at the same time, but would stop at the signal at the end of the platform until the way had been cleared to the locomotive depot. Pilot engines would bring outgoing stock into the terminus from the carriage sidings, uncouple at the buffer stops and would simmer there while the train engine was carefully backed down onto the stock. Once the express had departed then the pilot could run down the platform and be available for the next move to the carriage siding.

Trains that were running over shorter distances, or which could be adequately cleaned at the platform might be dealt with in a different way. In their case the pilot would be used to draw off the stock once the passengers had departed, allowing the incoming train engine to be released to go for coal, water and turning. The stock would then be propelled into the platform and the pilot detached, with another train engine replacing it in due course. Pilot engines were also employed in splitting sets and attaching extra coaches to long-distance trains and at one time spent much of their time dealing with mail and parcels vans.

Of course any move that involved a pilot engine took up a great deal of time and this method of operation became increasingly unsatisfactory in the busy city termini that were struggling to cope with millions of commuters each year. Liverpool Street was one of the worst affected as it dealt with far more suburban trains than expresses and had a huge number of trains to deal with during the rush hours. There a method of working evolved where incoming trains would run into » the station and the engine would be uncoupled as soon as possible. A fresh engine would be backed onto the stock immediately meaning that the train could be ready for departure again in as little as five minutes. Some pretty slick working arose from this practice and it was commonplace for the replacement engine to follow the stock down the platform and to be tied on just as soon as it had come to rest.

Turning engines in such circumstances would have been a luxury and so tank locomotives were universally employed on such duties with diagrams worked out so that coal and water was not always required at each visit to the terminus. Known as the 'Jazz Service', it was perhaps the most intensive steam-worked service anywhere in the world.

There were many terminus stations where trains arrived but were not at the end of their journey. One of these was Leeds Wellington where expresses from London would reverse before carrying on their journey to Scotland. In this case smart station work was required because the express was in effect only making a station stop.

A fresh express engine would be waiting in a convenient siding just outside the station and once the train was safely at a stand in the platform the replacement locomotive would be backed down to the rear of the stock and within minutes would depart. The original train engine would then be taken to the shed for servicing and would return to its own area at the head of a later train. In these cases no attempt was ever made to clean or service the train although the contents of the buffet car would be replenished if possible.

Country retreats

Life at a country terminus was somewhat more relaxed than it was in the major cities but unlike in the city stations those in the country also dealt with goods traffic. Mallaig in the West Highlands generated a massive quantity of fish traffic and passenger trains had to vie for space with fish vans and wagons bringing coal for the fishing

boats. Despite the remote location the station could host more than one locomotive at once and when the express fish trains were being made up there would be feverous shunting.

An interesting aspect of this type of branch was the running of mixed trains including vans full of fish being attached to the rear of expresses, all of which required complex shunting manoeuvres to get the wagons in the right place for loading while at the same time not delaying the passenger train. Branches in the West Country would also run mixed trains but in their case the tankers would be full of milk.

Steam-worked commuter services running into terminus stations proved inefficient and expensive to operate and in the areas with the highest commuter traffic ways of reducing the costs and improving efficiency were always being sought. In the south of England and in areas of the North West in the 1920s electrification schemes revolutionised the way that terminus stations handled traffic. With no separate locomotive to cater for there was no requirement for a pilot engine to haul stock to and from the station and trains could arrive and depart within minutes thanks to them being fitted with a driving cab at each end. At some locations, notably Waterloo, it became practice for a driver to be positioned at a point on the platform where the rear cab would come to rest so that the train could be readied for departure without waiting for the time that the original driver would have taken to walk its length. Such methods enabled trains to be utilised in a way that would have been impossible in earlier years.

The rest of the country had to wait many more years before steam was replaced by more modern traction but when it was the new diesel and electric locomotives were utilised in much the same way as had their steam counterparts. Trains arriving at termini still had a locomotive at the front and this had to be uncoupled from the train and then would remain trapped in at the buffer stops until either the station pilot took away the

The concourse of Southport Lord Street station on July 29 1951. Note the period advertisements ahead of the platforms. Simmering in the distance are '4F' 0-6-0 44285 and an Ivatt 2-6-0. Stan Garth/Rail Archive Stephenson.

The station pilot was an essential locomotive which would be busy shuffling carriages, vans and empty stock around a station. In 1956 Ivatt GNR 'N1' 0-6-2T 69447 waits to leave Leeds Central with empty stock. Kenneth Field/Rail Archive Stephenson.

coaches or more usually until the stock departed on its next working in the care of a fresh engine.

It became more common to service coaches in the terminus platforms and to use them more intensively and this reduced the work of the remaining station pilots, their duties then being confined to bringing fresh coaches from the carriage sidings at the start of each day or taking those back that needed either full servicing or storage until the next day.

Diesel-worked suburban services carried on the principle of a fresh engine being coupled as quickly as possible to an incoming train with intensive use of stock, but many services in the outer suburban and rural areas were turned over to Diesel Multiple Units which simply worked into and then out of a convenient platform and which could be sent back out in the time it took the driver to walk from one end to the other.

In the early-1970s when the new generation of high-speed trains was being planned it was realised that the economic case for such investment rested on a very high utilisation of stock being possible and key to this was the time that each train spent in a terminus station before it could be put back to work. Locomotives standing at the buffer stops or waiting for their next turn were not earning money and with this in mind both the High Speed Train and the Advanced Passenger Train were designed to have their locomotives

integral with their carriages and also to have a cab at each end. So successful was this principle that when locomotives such as the Class 91 were constructed special Driving Van Trailers were built to go with them so that they could be driven remotely from the opposite end of the train reducing wasted time.

Today almost all of the trains that visit our busy terminus stations are either fixed-formation multiple units or High Speed Trains which have a locomotive at each end. They provide a density of service that would have been unthinkable in steam days with turnaround times measured in mere minutes rather than hours. Electric Multiple Units serve most of the commuter network and glide silently in and out of platforms without needing any assistance from either shunter or pilot locomotive. While today's railway is certainly a colourful and busy place there are many who yearn for the days when a terminus saw a variety of movements much greater than we have now but which are sadly long gone. For the passenger though this pace of change is a revolution and now high availability of trains and rapid turn rounds are expected on a daily basis. Watching this unfold at one of Britain's great terminus stations is a great pleasure for different reasons, but for us as modellers the chance to recreate a busy transition era terminus is a great draw. ∎

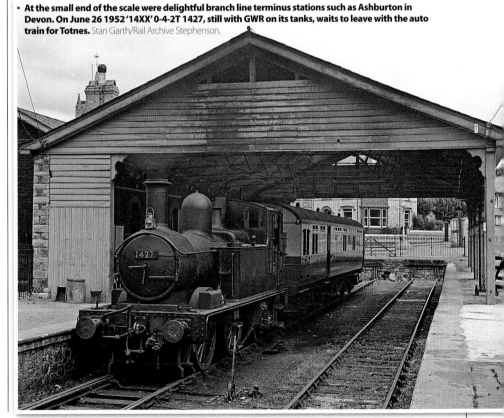

▪ **At the small end of the scale were delightful branch line terminus stations such as Ashburton in Devon. On June 26 1952 '14XX' 0-4-2T 1427, still with GWR on its tanks, waits to leave with the auto train for Totnes.** Stan Garth/Rail Archive Stephenson.

From Nebraska to the Black Country

Looking outside the usual sources for a building can reap big rewards. **TIM SHACKLETON** explains how Grosvenor Square's imposing terminus building came into being using an American outline kit as the basis.

IT WAS OBVIOUS from the start of this project that Grosvenor Square needed a station building reflecting the perceived importance of the city it served. We also wanted something that made a strong and dynamic visual statement on the layout. After considering any number of possibilities, we found the solution in the huge 'Cornerstone' range of 'HO' (3.5mm:1ft) scale structure kits from American company Wm K Walthers.

Union Station (Cat No. 933-3094) measures an impressive 20in x 9in x 7in (500mm x 230mm x 180mm) and is a scaled-down model of the former Burlington station in Omaha, Nebraska. It was opened in 1898 by the Chicago, Burlington & Quincy Railroad, and continued to handle passenger trains (latterly operated by

Amtrak) until it was replaced in 1974 by a much simpler structure. Burlington station still stands and is now used as a television studio.

So how do we get away with bringing an American 'HO' scale model into the context of a British layout built to 'OO' gauge (4mm:1ft)? In purely architectural terms, not all the kits available from companies such as Walthers and Design Preservation Models translate readily into a UK context but a key factor is that American model buildings are consistently so much larger than their British or European equivalents. Our manufacturers of structure kits and ready-to-plant models, I feel sure, seem to shrink buildings by anything up to 20% in a bid to allow more of them to fit into cramped British layouts. US modellers, on the other hand, seem to have much more space at their disposal and as a result their buildings are proportionately nearer a true scale size. This is why an 'HO' scale American building can look perfectly at home on an 'OO' gauge British outline railway – and Grosvenor Square station building, believe me, is nothing compared to

> *"We were struck by the kits resemblance to Huddersfield station."*
> **TIM SHACKLETON**

some of the large structures I've built for my own layout based on American kits.

Mike Wild and I were immediately struck by Union Station's resemblance to the Grade 1 listed railway station in Huddersfield, where both of us grew up. Building the model immediately took me back to steam days, when many a memorable spotting trip began by passing through the Grecian pillars that guarded the entrance. Opened in 1850, the station was sandblasted clean in the 1970s to reveal a frontage that was described by John Betjeman as 'the most splendid in England'.

Transferring our station building from the American Midwest to the West Midlands by way of the old West Riding of Yorkshire proved an interesting and rewarding exercise. A coat of soot and grime was the key ingredient – the actual assembly of the kit was straightforward, as so many of the Walthers products are, but I've described it here in some detail for the benefit of readers who may not be familiar with working on such large structures in 4mm scale. ∎

TOOLS & materials

- » Humbrol liquid poly
- » Limonene plastic cement
- » Loctite Power Flex superglue
- » Emery boards
- » Sanding sticks
- » Stanley knife
- » Xuron cutters
- » Sprue cutters
- » Craft knife
- » Corner clamps
- » Plastic clamps
- » Squadron green putty
- » Airbrush
- » Humbrol detail brushes

This style of classical architecture can be found pretty well all over the world and it requires but little imagination to translate this American kit into a British railway station. The etched sign is the clincher but the general air of down-at-heel urban decrepitude is very much a product of the way it was painted.

STEP BY STEP **ANGLICISING AN AMERICAN STONE STATION BUILDING**

Intermediate
Beginner **SKILL LEVEL** Advanced

1 If you're used to the modest size (in relation to high cost) of many British and European kits, the sheer magnitude and affordability of some of these American plastic models may come as a surprise. Healthy sales on the home market ensure UK modellers buying these kits benefit from economies of scale.

2 The components are crisply moulded and while the detailing might be considered basic, there is plenty of scope for additions and improvements if you're so minded. Thanks to advanced design and quality-conscious manufacturing technology, everything fits together beautifully.

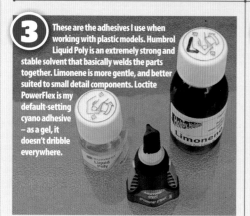

3 These are the adhesives I use when working with plastic models. Humbrol Liquid Poly is an extremely strong and stable solvent that basically welds the parts together. Limonene is more gentle, and better suited to small detail components. Loctite PowerFlex is my default-setting cyano adhesive – as a gel, it doesn't dribble everywhere.

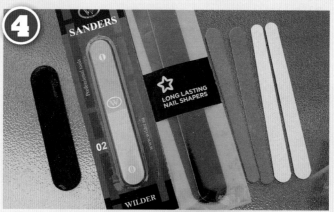

4 For as long as I can remember (and I first started building plastic kits in the late 1950s) I've used emery board nail files when working with plastic. When they eventually clog and lose their bite – as they will – I throw them away and use a new one. A worn file won't give you a smooth surface so instead I use fine-grade sanding sticks of anything up to 4000 grit.

5 Cutting tools for working with plastic – a Stanley knife, Xuron cutters, sprue cutters (for nipping small parts from the moulding sprue) and a craft knife with an extremely sharp blade.

6 I begin assembly by using the side cutters to remove the main components. A Stanley knife does just as well but there's more risk of damaging yourself.

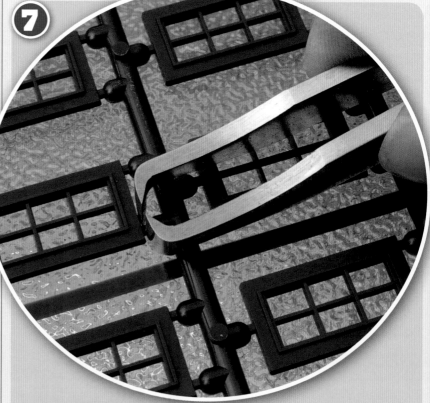

7 Sprue cutters, though very powerful, are more precise in action and the pincer movement means parts are unlikely to snap when being snipped off.

uddersfield station, seen here in the 1950s (note the trolleybus wires) was my main inspiration but I was lso influenced by the general design of Aberystwyth and Cardiff General.

USEFUL LINKS

Lifecolor	www.airbrushes.com
Humbrol products	www.humbrol.co.uk
Walthers kits	www.gaugemaster.com

8 I used liberal amounts of Liquid Poly to get the walls erected on the base. To ensure they're square and vertical I used a heavy box as a support, bracing the assembly from the other side with my cutters. After ten minutes or so the joints will have set sufficiently hard for the workpiece to be safely handled.

9 Your fingers are an amazing tool for holding parts in exact alignment but these adjustable clamps do much the same job. Their padded jaws ensure the plastic components aren't scratched or damaged in any way. Mine came from The Right Clamp Company in the USA – various sizes and designs are available.

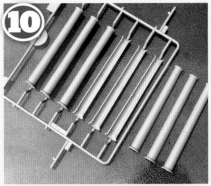

10 I pre-assembled the columns at the front of the building so I could more easily file the joins smooth. Good design ensures a near-perfect fit with minimal gaps.

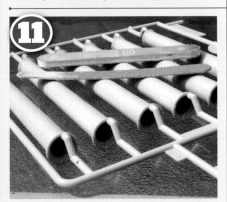

11 Once assembled and smoothed off, the columns can be kept in their sprue ready for painting. On the finished model they'll be tight up against the front wall and painting would be difficult.

12 The most useful modelling tools I own are these blocks of oak that I obtained many years ago as offcuts from a cabinet maker. I knew they'd been planed truly square so they're useful in all kinds of modelling applications – here, I'm using them as alignment aids.

13 The upper walls of the main building come in two sections, front and rear. These plastic clamps keep them aligned while the adhesive sets.

CONSTRUCTION

STEP BY STEP | ANGLICISING AN AMERICAN STONE STATION BUILDING

Intermediate
Beginner | SKILL LEVEL | Advanced

14

Using clamps and other alignment aids ensures the assembly is square and true. All the same I check that everything is as it should be before going off to make a cup of tea. Liquid Poly is strong stuff and once it's dried, separating misaligned wall sections can be difficult.

15

Amid a sea of discarded sprues, the main form of the building starts to emerge. What pleases me is that everything went together perfectly, at the first time of asking. Nothing needed modifying or filing to fit, and the mitred corners were particularly good.

16

There were very minor gaps at the tops of the walls, which I filled using Squadron green putty. Being flat, a blunt craft-knife blade acts like a spatula and is an ideal application tool. Once hardened off, the filler can be sanded smooth.

18

17

I airbrushed the basic shell using two warm shades of brownish-black – predominantly Worn Black (734) but with strong hints of Burned Black (738), both from Lifecolor. I made no attempt to achieve a 100% even coverage, allowing the underlying beige of the plastic to show through in places.

THE PAINT CODES		
UA734 Worn Black	Lifecolor	
UA738 Burned Black	Lifecolor	
UA722 Roof Dirt	Lifecolor	
UA706 Dust Type 2	Lifecolor	
1260 Dullcote	Testors	

I airbrushed the columns with the same colours, creating gentle modulations of tone. The airbrush is an Iwata Revolution CR, which is great for applying considerable volumes of paint as well as subtle blending. I am very sparing with the amount of paint I put on and used less than two cupfuls to paint the entire station structure!

19

The window frames were brush-painted while still on their sprues, then given a gentle waft of weathering to tone down the intensity. Pure white was uncommon until the late-1960s, so I used a creamy-grey colour that Lifecolor helpfully labels as 'Dust Type 2'.

20

Once the columns guarding the entrance are in place, this really starts to look like a place of considerable importance – if a little down on its luck these days.

21

The roofs slot into position from underneath and are retained by a fillet of cyano running round the inside of the parapet walls. Throughout the build I was impressed by the exactness of fit, even with a structure on such an epic scale.

The Walthers building is based on Burlington station in Omaha, Nebraska, seen here from the platform side.

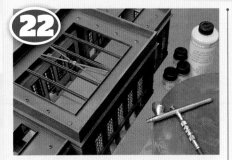

22 I painted the roofs with another Lifecolor shade called, happily enough, Roof Dirt (UA722). It's intended for rolling stock but I thought it did very well for the textured surfaces on the main roofs of the station building. Once again I went for a thin, slightly uneven coat applied at a high pressure to avoid spattering.

23 The glass in skylights and platform canopies doesn't gleam like a shop window. It's flat and opaque, represented in this before-and-after shot by a double coat of Testor's Dullcote – a near indispensable American lacquer spray that gives a perfect matt finish to almost any surface.

24 Next, I run in a thin dark wash along the glazing bars to pick out relief detail and add a measure of discoloration. I'm fussy about the brushes I use but I like the Humbrol 'Detail' range both for their quality – they keep their shape very well – and the comfortable handles.

25 To suggest replacement glass, I painted the rear of some of the panes with a variety of pale grey washes. We see a lot of our models from above and it pays to make an effort with these things.

26 The sign was custom-etched and after priming was discoloured with well-thinned acrylic paints. The brush is clearly on its way out but is still useful for this kind of thing.

27 The *Hornby Magazine* team were so pleased with the way I'd built and painted the model that I was given the plum job of building an overall roof to match. The station is taking shape.

A tale of two 'Panniers'

GWR 'Pannier' tanks are perennial favourites and Bachmann has added the '64XX' version to its existing 'OO' gauge range. **PAUL CHETTER** investigates the installation of sound and 'stay alive' capability to this and the earlier '57XX' series locomotives.

DESPITE BEING of superficially similar outward appearance, there are significant internal differences between these two models of GWR '57XX' and '64XX' 0-6-0PTs. This guide will help you whichever model you have. Although the Zimo MX649 sound decoder and 15mm x 11mm x 9mm 'cube' speaker can be fitted to each model, the design changes dictate that they must be installed differently.

In fact, the only similarities between these installations is that the Digital Command Control (DCC) interface was removed from each model and the insulating sheath plus unused wires were removed from the decoders, all to create enough space for the full workings of sound. Both are DCC ready, but there is not a great deal of free space available for components beyond non-sound decoder installation.

The '57XX'

In order to remove the '57XX' model's body from its chassis, the tension lock couplings must be removed then the revealed screws front and rear released. After lifting the body clear it can be seen that the chassis is equipped with an 8-pin DCC socket on a small Printed Circuit Board (PCB) which dominates the boiler space in front of the motor.

Crucially, the U shaped ballast weight fitted in the pannier and smokebox voids has a cut out section in the right-hand tank. This is sufficient to accommodate a miniature sound decoder like the 2016 introduced Zimo MX649. When the DCC socket has been removed and its supporting pillars snipped off the resulting space can be used to accept the speaker without modification, a couple of 25v 330µF capacitors wired in series plus the diode and resistor required to control in-rush current.

Although removing the DCC interface requires the decoder to be hard wired to the pick-up and motor wires, this results in all of the added components being completely hidden from view after reassembly and the sound emanating from the forward portion of the model. I suggest that you do not drill out the chimney as its structural integrity will be seriously compromised. Surprisingly, there is no need to create a pathway to free air as the speaker works more effectively when fully enclosed.

The 660µF 'stay alive' capacitance available will not provide substantial wheel rotation and should be considered more as an aid to keeping the decoder operating during momentary power disruptions or 'brown outs' where high resistance (such as from dirty track) causes temporary voltage drops.

The higher capacitance of Zimo's SC68 supercapacitor (6800µF) in a compact package would enable a small but visible part rotation of the wheels to clear minor electrical gaps. There is no space available in the boiler for this so it would need to be fitted in the cab where it would be visible from some viewing angles.

The '64XX'

The front tension lock coupling must be removed to reveal the forward body to chassis securing screw as before but the rear screw is in plain sight, slightly forward of the rear coupling position.

With the body removed, the changes to the chassis are apparent. The PCB has been relocated to the front of the lower boiler

STEP BY STEP INSTALLING SOUND AND 'STAY ALIVE' CAPABILITY IN A BACHMANN '57XX'

1 The cutaway picture shows the small amount of usable space within the boiler. The internal design of both locomotives is similar, although the '57XX' uses an 8-pin socket while the '64XX' has a 6-pin socket.

casting and mounted vertically. The DCC socket is a 6-pin version allowing direct plug-in decoders to be fitted to the upper portion of the boiler space. In view of this, the U-shaped ballast weight no longer features a cutout section to house the decoder.

There are a couple of ways that a sound decoder and speaker can be deployed in this configuration but neither of them will enable 'stay alive' capacitors to be fitted here. Any such capacitance must be accommodated in the cab.

The design also incorporates changes to the cab moulding, in particular the provision of a cab floor and boiler backhead which seal off the cab space from the rest of the model. This presents a problem as access to the cab space is limited to and by the size of the openings above the cab doors.

I found that a 25v 1000µF capacitor would pass through these openings and fit transversely on the floor of the cab. Some black insulating tape and matt black paint will effectively conceal its presence but it could be further disguised by adding suitably adapted model footplate crew.

The MX649N direct 6-pin decoder can be installed in the DCC socket as intended in the model's design. The space below the fitted decoder is shallow and the green coloured inductors fitted to the PCB compromise what little space there is available. It would be possible to use the DCC socket and fit the speaker into the cab, but a degree of modification would be required to gain access to the cab space.

Alternatively, the DCC socket could be used with the speaker fitted below the decoder. In order to achieve this, however, the speaker enclosure would need to be drastically reduced in height to match the space available. In this case I would suggest removing the top of the enclosure, filing down the enclosure walls until a fit is possible, then glue the speaker 'upside down' onto the chassis to form a sealed

enclosure again.

Taking all these issues into account I decided to remove the PCB, DCC socket and inductors and hardwire an MX649 sound decoder. The decoder is short enough to fit without modifying the chassis and is sufficiently narrow to fit side-on between body and chassis. By locating the decoder to one side of the boiler enough space becomes available for an unmodified cube speaker plus the diode and resistor for the 'stay alive' capacitor in-rush current protection.

A small hole must be drilled for the wires from the decoder to pass through to the 'stay alive' capacitor located in the cab in such a location as to keep the wires from view in the cab and from fouling the motor or wheels forward of the cab. In this case, I reassembled the model before finally fitting the capacitor. ∎

WHAT WE USED		
Product	**Supplier**	**Price**
Zimo MX649 Sound Decoder (two)	www.digitrains.co.uk	£92.00
Zimo 8mm x 12mm cube speaker (two)	www.digitrains.co.uk	£9.50

Two 'Panniers' modelling two different classes, but with similar requirements for installing digital sound. Paul Chetter explains how in this step by step guide.

STEP BY STEP **INSTALLING SOUND AND 'STAY ALIVE' CAPABILITY IN A BACHMANN '57XX'**

2

Remove the tension lock couplings for access to the body securing screws, arrowed. These should be released allowing the body to lift straight upwards and off.

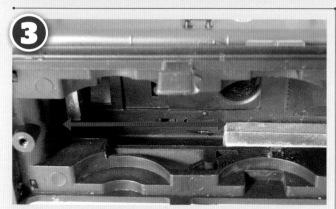

3

This view of the inside of the body moulding shows the cutout provided to house a small decoder in one of the pannier tank weights.

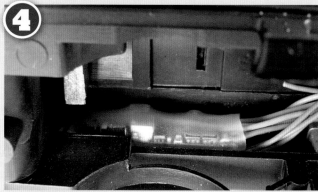

4

During a 'dry run' the Zimo MX649 can be seen fitting comfortably within this space even with the standard insulating sleeve in place. This sleeve will be removed to allow access to the solder pads.

5

The standard PCB and 8-pin DCC socket dominate the otherwise free space within the boiler. I removed the two screws holding the PCB in place. Note that in this model the orange wire is to the left-hand side of the motor and grey to the right.

6

Then I unsoldered the red and black track pick-up wires and removed the orange and grey connection wires from the motor. I used a pair of side cutting pliers to remove the PCB mounting pillars to create a larger space with a flat lower surface.

8 With the sheath removed there is easy access to the solder pads. I added a grey wire to the lower right solder pad for the Ground connection. The grey wire connects to the negative lead of the capacitors.

7

The capacitor charging control circuit consists of a series resistor and a diode, the anode of which should be connected to the positive lead on the capacitors. The anode is the end without a painted bar, in this picture the right-hand side. This is a compact package which will sit above and between the capacitors.

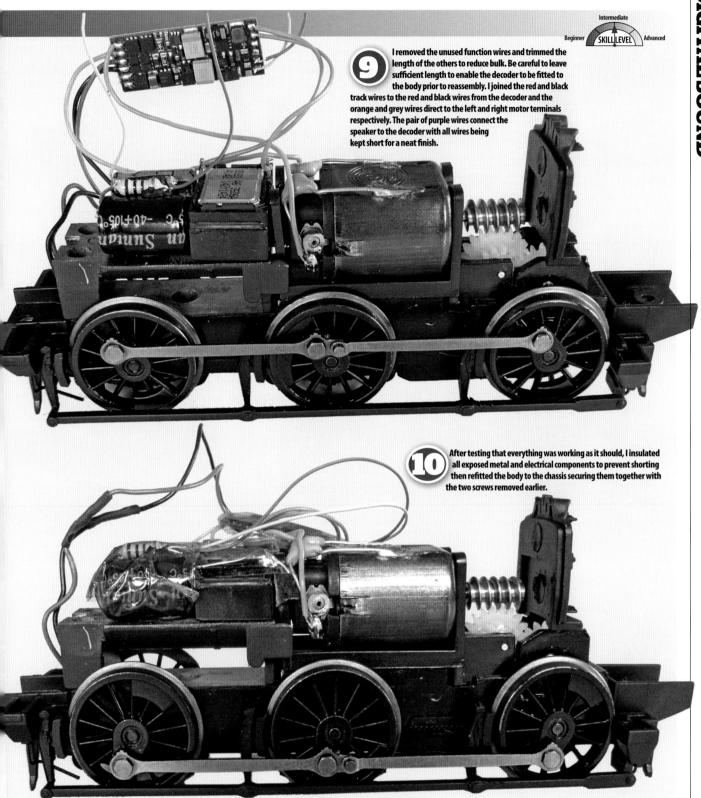

9 I removed the unused function wires and trimmed the length of the others to reduce bulk. Be careful to leave sufficient length to enable the decoder to be fitted to the body prior to reassembly. I joined the red and black track wires to the red and black wires from the decoder and the orange and grey wires direct to the left and right motor terminals respectively. The pair of purple wires connect the speaker to the decoder with all wires being kept short for a neat finish.

10 After testing that everything was working as it should, I insulated all exposed metal and electrical components to prevent shorting then refitted the body to the chassis securing them together with the two screws removed earlier.

'Stay alive' capacitors and 'in-rush' current

If large capacitance either in one model or as a result of combining the values of several models with smaller capacitors are allowed to charge freely, there will be a resulting surge in power requirement or 'in-rush' current. DCC controllers may falsely detect this as a short circuit, resulting in the system shutting down for protection.

To avoid this, some Zimo decoders have in-built circuitry to control it. The miniature decoders do not and so a solution similar to that of other decoder brands is described in the Zimo manual. A wired connection should be made between the decoder's Ground solder pad and the capacitor's Negative terminal.

A series resistor is incorporated into the connection between the Common Positive output of the decoder and the Positive terminal of the capacitor. This reduces the rate of charging and the 'in-rush' current possible.

When the decoder requires the capacitor to provide power it would be counter-productive to force the flow back through the resistor, and so a diode is fitted in parallel allowing instant and full current discharge via this alternative pathway.

Note that this simple circuit does not limit voltage and so the capacitor's working voltage must be higher than the track; 25v or 35v may be required. The result is a highly effective 'stay alive' system.

STEP BY STEP **INSTALLING DCC SOUND AND 'STAY ALIVE' IN A BACHMANN '64XX'**

A This cutaway picture shows the revised gearbox arrangements and PCB position of this more recently designed model.

B The front retaining screw is revealed when the tension lock coupling has been removed. The rear screw, however, is in plain sight slightly forward of the rear coupling. The screws are arrowed.

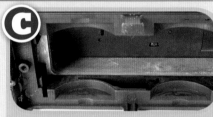

C The redesigned decoder socket removes the need for a cut out in the U-shaped ballast weight inside the pannier tanks. This space restriction results in the 'stay alive' capacitor being housed in the cab space.

D The MX649 direct 6-pin decoder will fit the DCC socket and the space provided. Note that in this model, the grey wire is soldered to the left-hand motor connection and the orange wire to the right.

E It is not possible to fit a cube speaker without modifying it in the free space below the decoder. If you wish to use this configuration, the height of the speaker enclosure must be reduced to fit the space and a sealed enclosure formed by gluing it to the chassis.

F I decided to remove the PCB and motor connection wiring in order to hardwire the decoder.

G The MX649 is supplied with a heatshrink insulating sheath which I removed to reduce bulk and gain access to the solder pads.

H I removed the unused function wires and added blue (positive) and grey (ground) to the two lower pads on the right of the picture.

I With the decoder orientated side-on to the chassis, there is sufficient room to fit an as delivered cube speaker.

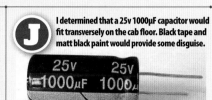

J I determined that a 25v 1000µF capacitor would fit transversely on the cab floor. Black tape and matt black paint would provide some disguise.

K The diode and resistor package was made as compact as possible to fit behind the speaker and alongside the MX649. I used black wires to connect to the capacitor as the rear ends will be passed through into the cab space. I used the convention 'long lead is the positive lead' to ensure correct polarity when connecting the capacitor later.

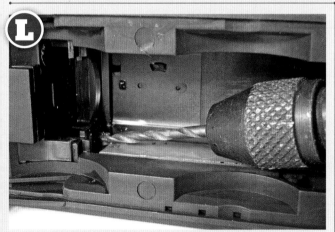

L I drilled a small hole in the left-hand side of the boiler backhead to allow the wires to pass from the decoder to capacitor in the cab space.

M To avoid making bulky wiring joints I soldered the red and black track wires directly to the decoder and the orange and grey wires from the decoder directly to the motor terminals.

N A programme of insulation was undertaken to prevent shorting when reassembled.

O After refitting the body and securing it to the chassis with the two screws removed earlier, I soldered the wires to the capacitor. I insulated with black tape which helps to disguise the capacitor's presence in the cab. Adding a crew will further hide its presence in the cab.

Building platforms

There is a myriad of methods and materials which can be used to make model platforms. **MIKE WILD** explains how with a combination of timber, plastic, card, resin and ballast the extensive platforms for Grosvenor Square were built in 'OO' scale.

Four separate platforms make up the seven faces of Grosvenor Square. The surface is Slater's embossed plasticard with mounting card, MDF and Redutex brick textures making up the underlying parts.

EVERY TIME we catch a train we stand on the platforms, but how often have we actually taken note of how they are built? Personally, platform construction is one of my least favourite occupations when it comes to layout construction – I'd much rather be under the layout wiring it up and burning my fingers. That said, a model like Grosvenor Square really can't be without a decent set of platforms.

There are a lot of choices when it comes to model platforms. Kits, ready-made and scratchbuilding are the main options, but within that there are choices of material including timber, plastic and card. Kits can be useful while ready-made structures are quick to install but limited in their flexibility.

For this layout the only real option was a multi-media scratchbuilding project, but using methods which should make it relatively quick to erect the four platforms serving seven tracks. The basis is 12mm Medium Density Fibreboard (MDF) which is cheap to buy and easy to cut. It also gives good clean edges which is very useful for adding facing to the platform edges. However, there isn't a depth of MDF available which gives the perfect height for platforms, so we have raised the total depth to 16mm with two layers of 1/16in cork.

Edging is cut from sheets of Redutex brick sheeting

WHAT WE USED		
Product	Source	Cat No.
12mm Medium Density Fibreboard	DIY store	
1/16in cork sheet	Gaugemaster	
2.0mm thick mounting card	Hobby store	
Embossed plasticard, paving	Slaters	0414
Flexible embossed pre-coloured brick sheets	Redutex	076LD112
Medium Sea Grey acrylic	Tamiya	XF-83
Rain marks wash acrylic	Lifecolor	LPW11
Matt varnish	Humbrol	49
Fine blended grey ballast	Woodland Scenics	B1393
Medium blended grey ballast	Woodland Scenics	B1394

– a wonderful material range which consists of ready coloured self-adhesive flexible resin sheets which can be cut to shape and applied in minutes. These have been a tremendous help in getting the base structure completed in a timely fashion.

Topping the base is 2mm thick mounting card covered with Slater's embossed plasticard. This has been cut into strips for the edges and panels for the centres before being treated to a triple coating of paints using Tamiya Medium Sea Grey, Lifecolor Rainmarks wash and Humbrol acrylic matt varnish.

The completed platforms are all capable of hosting a six coach train – two will hold six plus a parcels van – and are now ready for the finishing touches. The step by step guide explains how we built the platforms from the ground up. ■

CONSTRUCTION

STEP BY STEP **BUILDING PLATFORMS FOR GROSVENOR SQUARE**

TOOLS and glues

» Handsaw
» Tape measure
» Steel ruler
» Pencil
» Craft knife
» Scissors
» Contact adhesive
» PVA wood glue

1 The basis of the platforms is 12mm MDF, but unfortunately it isn't quite the right height and there isn't 16mm MDF available from stores! However, it cuts easily and is relatively cheap too. We used two 4ft x 2ft sheets to build these platforms.

2

TIP

Large platforms can be a big job to tackle, but by selecting simple materials which could cover large areas quickly their impact in the build time was reduced. Redutex brick texture sheets give a quick, clean and simple finish to their faces.

All of the straight sections of platform and the area underneath the station building were cut to size first and laid out on the layout. Any adjustments were then made prior to the final sections for the ends and ramps being cut to length.

3 To begin raising the height of the platform base, 1/16in cork sheet was laid underneath – this was a simple, quick and effective means of achieving small height increases.

4 With a brick face positioned against the now 14mm deep platform base, trains were positioned in the platforms to gauge their height. Diagnosis: they were still too low.

Suitably painted in stone grey colours and with use of Lifecolor washes the platforms are starting to look the part. Detailing is next.

5 Another layer of cork was layered on top of the MDF base next to add a further 2mm to the overall height of the platform bases which for us turned out to be just about perfect.

6 Redutex brick sheets, a self-adhesive moulded and pre-coloured resin material, were cut into 15mm deep strips to make the platform edging – a process which took a little over an hour to edge the entire platform area.

7 Next the surfaces were cut from 2mm thick mounting card taking care to ensure adequate clearance for rolling stock moving in and out of the station.

CONSTRUCTION

STEP BY STEP **BUILDING PLATFORMS FOR GROSVENOR SQUARE**

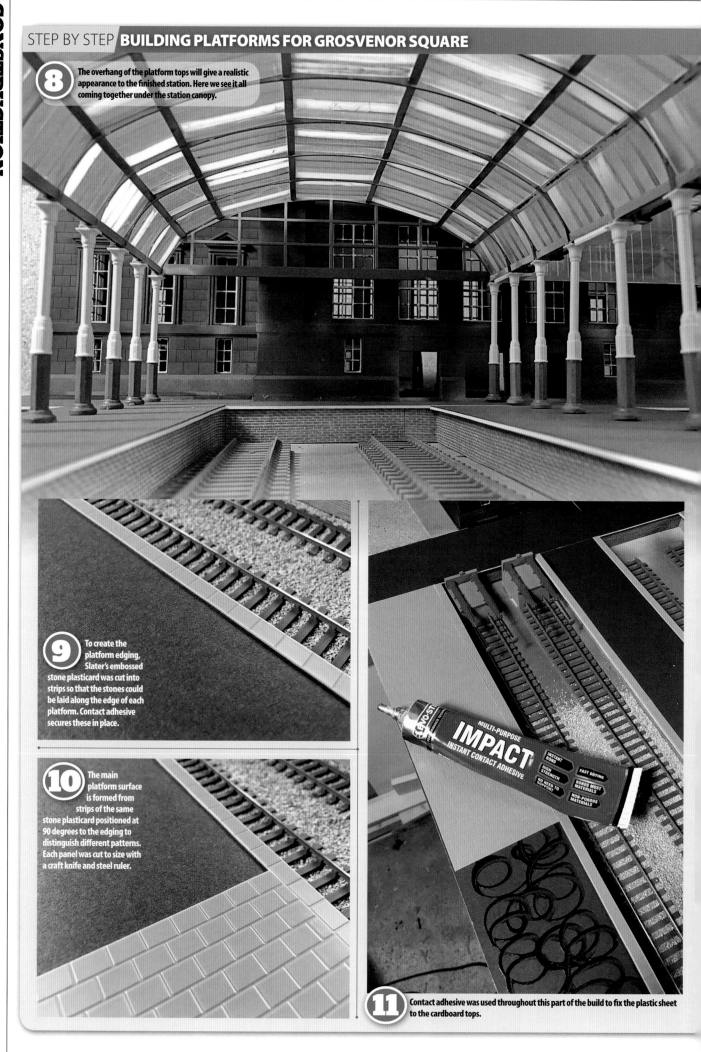

8 The overhang of the platform tops will give a realistic appearance to the finished station. Here we see it all coming together under the station canopy.

9 To create the platform edging, Slater's embossed stone plasticard was cut into strips so that the stones could be laid along the edge of each platform. Contact adhesive secures these in place.

10 The main platform surface is formed from strips of the same stone plasticard positioned at 90 degrees to the edging to distinguish different patterns. Each panel was cut to size with a craft knife and steel ruler.

11 Contact adhesive was used throughout this part of the build to fix the plastic sheet to the cardboard tops.

12 To allow the card to bend neatly at the ends of the platforms a triangular notch was scribed in the rear 80mm from the end.

13 This was then overlaid with embossed plasticard in the same way with the plastic being scribed to follow the bend for the ramp too.

14 After several hours of cutting and shaping plasticard, the platform surfaces were complete. To create a neat edge with the station build the plasticard sheets go underneath the rear of the building so no joins are apparent.

15 Colouring starts with a thinned coat of Tamiya Medium Sea Grey acrylic (XF-83) applied by brush. It was thinned with acrylic thinners to make application quicker and easier.

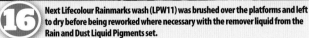

16 Next Lifecolour Rainmarks wash (LPW11) was brushed over the platforms and left to dry before being reworked where necessary with the remover liquid from the Rain and Dust Liquid Pigments set.

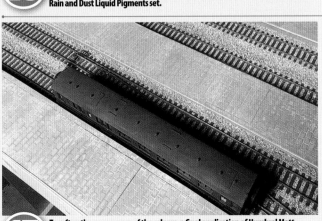

17 To soften the appearance of the colours, a final application of Humbrol Matt Varnish (49) was sprayed over the platforms readying them for final weathering and detailing.

18 Finally the platforms were glued down to the bases using contact adhesive and the final section of the rear platform was filled with Woodland Scenics blended grey ballast secured in place with PVA glue to give this area a different look.

MasTe

SYDNEY GARDENS in Bath is amongst the most famous of railway locations. The stone walled cutting has been the back drop to thousands of photographs taken from the lineside parkland. The group known as the Park Keepers – a bunch of friends located in Wiltshire – saw an opportunity to recreate this stretch of railway in 'OO'

gauge with their model making its debut on the exhibition circuit in 2015 – including an appearance at the Hornby Magazine sponsored Great Electric Train Show. Modelling a typical late 1950s scene a GWR 'King' 4-6-0 leads a rake of matching Western Region chocolate and cream Mk 1s through Sydney Gardens. Sydney Gardens featured in HM102.

Trevor Jones/*Hornby Magazine.*

With more than 500 images to choose from and covering almost 40 layouts selecting those to appear in this Gallery is always a tough challenge. *Hornby Magazine* presents a small selection of the best layout photographs from 2016.

pieces in the Gallery

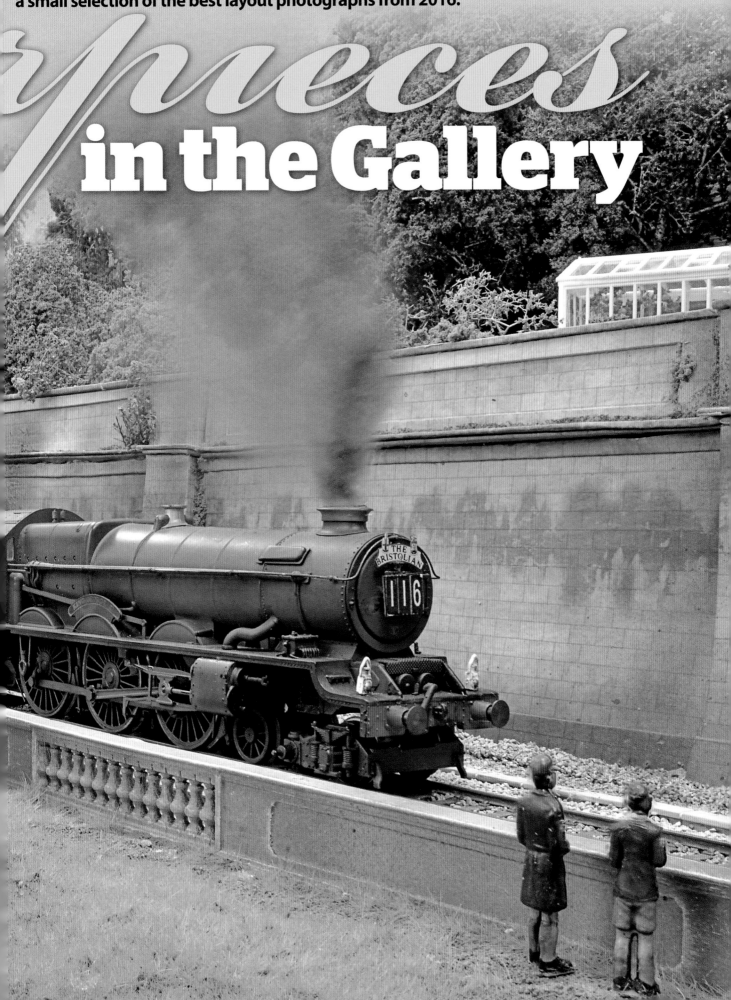

OLD ELMS ROAD models a location where regions meet – the perfect excuse for modellers with varied tastes to run rolling stock from more than one area of the country. With its mix of Western and Southern region motive power, not forgetting a third-rail electrified branch from the Southern and a second Western branch line, it packs a great deal of operational potential into this busy main line centred exhibition layout. At the station throat a Bulleid rebuilt 'Merchant Navy' 4-6-2 is ready to depart as a North British Type 2 hydraulic from the Western Region pilots a 'Hall' at the head of a heavy Travelling Post Office working. Wonderful nostalgia. Old Elms Road featured in HM105. Trevor Jones/Hornby Magazine.

PENHALLICK was a star performer on the exhibition circuit at every outing with its massive 56ft long frontage always drawing a crowd. In 2011 the 'OO' layout was retired for a new life as a permanent railway in a purpose built building where its owners took the opportunity to expand and develop the layout for a long term future. However, the admirable qualities of the original terminus station were kept as the starting point for the newly developed version including the charming town scene extension beyond the end of the line. Penhallick, in its new form, featured in HM101. *Trevor Jones/Hornby Magazine.*

PAUL WADE'S TONBRIDGE WEST YARD was a star of the 1990s exhibition circuit and, after a short interlude, it returned to the public domain in 2015 with appearances including the *Hornby Magazine* sponsored Great Electric Train Show. This busy 'OO' gauge layout models the engineering yard at Tonbridge together with the passing main line. Paul has invested thousands of hours building detailed scenes both on and off the railway and, perhaps most noticeably, in developing a stunning array of engineering vehicles from the early 1990s. At the entrance to the yard a Class 09 diesel shunter propels loaded ballast hoppers in to the yard as a Class 33/0 in 'Dutch' grey and yellow departs with a rake of Satlink liveried wagons. Tonbridge West Yard featured in HM103.
Trevor Jones/Hornby Magazine.

NEWTON CENTRAL is the first half of Andy Statham's developing 'OO' gauge home layout which models a combined through and terminus station set on former Great Central Railway metals in the Sheffield area. Using memories from his childhood Andy set out to model a location with his skills in military and card modelling as the first steps. Fully digital controlled and incorporating a number of sound equipped locomotives it serves as an evocative reminder of the hard working railway network in South Yorkshire in the 1950s and early 1960s. Newton Central featured in HM108. *Mike Wild/Hornby Magazine.*

OFFICE

GAS & COKE C°

STATHAM & Sons

BUILDERS MERCHANTS

&CONTRACTORS

Tel: Newton 79717   Est: 1935

63601

began life as a depot scene, but has since grown – and grown several more times, at the hands of its owner Allan Cromarty, to feature a terminus station, through lines, a cement terminal, oil depot and more. This 'OO' layout has become highly popular on the exhibition circuit too and was one of 25 layouts to attend the 2016 Great Electric Train Show at the British Motor Museum. By night a flock of Class 47s are illuminated by the yard towers with low relief industrial units forming the backdrop. Oulton TMD featured in HM107. *Trevor Jones/Hornby Magazine.*

BR'S WESTERN REGION hydraulics have always been a great draw for enthusiasts and modellers alike – even for Scotland-based Keith Sully who wanted to recreate holidays in the West Country, as he remembered them in the early 1970s, in 'OO'. A BR maroon 'Western' draws into Bere Banks with a rake of freshly painted BR blue and grey Mk 1 stock capturing a daily scene from the first years of the 1970s. Bere Banks featured in HM112.
Nigel Burkin/Hornby Magazine.

THE 2FT GAUGE Ffestiniog Railway in North Wales was the inspiration for David John's Rhyd. Modelled in 'O-14' scale this stunning and colourful recreation of the famous Welsh slate railway captures a small through station which is served by a fantastically varied range of narrow locomotives. Between the famous Double Fairlie and George England locomotives there are also delightful industrial shunters including Baldwin 2-4-0 diesel *Moelwyn* which joined the Ffestiniog fleet in 1925. Rhyd featured in HM101.
Nigel Burkin/Hornby Magazine.

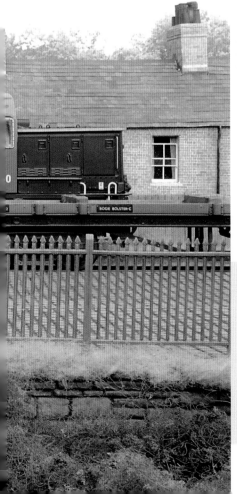

THE FOREST OF DEAN became the inspiration for Paul Marshall-Potter's ever evolving exhibition layout Albion Yard which captures the feel of the rural railways which once ran into the forest during the early 1960s. A Class 14 diesel-hydraulic ticks over in the headshunt having arrived with a rake of 14ton tankers from the tar works as a local parcels delivery van heads back out to the main road. Albion Yard featured in HM107.
Mike Wild/Hornby Magazine.

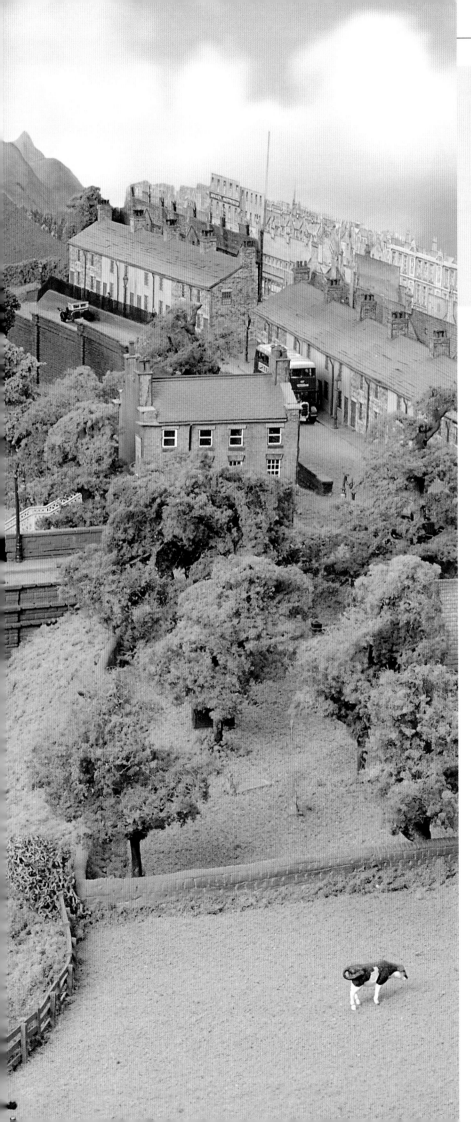

ANDY CALVERT was a leading light in modern 'N' gauge modelling techniques and especially when he debuted this wonderful LMS theme layout Calverdale in the late 1980s. It is now in the care of John Warner and remains fully operational as lasting memory of the work that Andy did for scale both in direct modelling terms and as the leading light in the N Gauge Society's kit programme. Calverdale has moved forward in time by 20 years to reflect BR operations – as shown by a Graham Farish Thompson 'B1' 4-6-0 leading an express through the station. Calverdale featured in HM110.
Mike Wild/Hornby Magazine.

Low relief

RAILWAY STATIONS were often squeezed onto tight plots of land in city environments, having to find space between business and private property. For a city terminus like Grosvenor Square, recreating that feeling of the railway being confined by its surroundings is an important step.

Early in the build we established ideas for different types of backdrop and buildings that we wanted to incorporate, but with just over 3in of depth to play with there wasn't going to be much room for anything. That's where the idea of low relief, or part relief, buildings come into play. They add a three dimensional look to a backscene without the need for full depth buildings which, in the case of this layout, could have added at least another foot to the width of the baseboards.

Having established that low relief was the way to go we sketched out a handful of ideas which showed buildings of different depths and with different purposes along the rear edge of the layout. The primary structures would be a station

hotel behind the station building, a large factory complex and a part relief road behind a retaining wall. On plotting out the scene we added a second factory and a small area of inner city parkland to add a little colour and foliage to the otherwise industrial scene.

Now we needed buildings and with the station and canopy being so big, whatever we chose needed to be able to compete in size so that it didn't become dwarfed. The first structure selected for the backdrop was the Walthers Champion Packing Plant – not least because it was already in the office from a previous project idea.

However, it wasn't designed as a low relief structure as delivered so it was going to need modification. The kit builds a 12in x 8in main building, a chimney and a second smaller boiler house together with conveyor runs and loading docks. Even though it wasn't designed as a low relief structure, with modification it was quickly turned into three frontages with the largest being 2ft 9in long using the two long sides and one end from the main building. The other smaller building

was cut in two in a two-thirds to one-third ratio to create another pair of structures meaning that the Packing Plant kit would now fill almost 4ft of the backdrop. That meant there was only another 8ft to go.

Painting of the packing plant was taken care of by Lifecolor acrylics with its Rainmarks wash (LPW11) being used for the mortar course followed by dry brushing of its Worn Brick (UA737) and Old Tile (UA740) colour over the top. The concrete sections were finished with Lifecolor BR Freight Grey (UA818).

Because of the changes to the structure, a little filling was necessary at the joins between the main wall sections using Humbrol filler while the original roof moulding was now no good for the new format. To replace this we used 2.5mm thick mounting card spray painted with Railmatch Roof Dirt colouring.

This collection of buildings has become the centerpiece to the backdrop and gives a sizeable structure to rival the station in size. To further

Creating a backdrop to a railway scene doesn't have to rely on printed or painted backscenes. **MIKE WILD** explains how the low relief scene at the back of Grosvenor Square developed.

The station hotel is viewed across the station roof together with trees from the city park.

Above left: Views like this are where low relief structures come into their own. Looking through the station it is difficult to discern what is there, but that is part of the aim – nothing in the background should shout or scream, but quite simply blend in with its surroundings.

Below: The power of low relief buildings is demonstrated here as 'Castle' 7029 *Clun Castle* departs Platform 7 with a rake of chocolate and cream BR Mk 1s. The 'Packing Plant' dominates the background, but other buildings and the parkland add to the sense of depth in the distance.

detail the backdrop we decided to add a very low relief – 5mm deep – factory building using foamboard covered with Redutex weathered brick 3D texture sheets to finish it. This covers a baseboard joint neatly too with one of the three roof pitches to the right of the joint and the other two to the left.

Parks and hotels

A small gap follows the 'super low relief' factory before the parkland. A frame cut from 2.5mm thick mounting card was made first and covered with Redutex red brick 3D textures followed by a raised ground level set behind the card using foamboard.

To add detail to this the foamboard was spray painted brown first with Humbrol No. 29 aerosol before the addition of a path with Woodland Scenics fine blended grey ballast, fine turfs from Greenscene and a collection of bushes from the MiniNatur range. Park benches by Noch complete

the scene together with a handful of sea moss trees raided from a previous layout project.

Behind the station we wanted to introduce a hotel building. Height was important and while there are options available off the shelf we were looking to keep the buildings on Grosvenor Square more bespoke. A search on the internet showed that Metcalfe Models' department store would be just the ticket and we used one full kit and a third of a second kit to create the three bay building which sits behind the station. The interiors have been omitted and to avoid it drawing the eye it has been finished without signage.

This building was a pleasure to build and the construction methods employed in it create a rigid building with plenty of detail. Weathering with Lifecolor Burned Black (UA736) – the same colour as the station building - completed the model making it ready to install in place on the layout. »

The final section

So far we had filled 8ft out of the 12ft of backdrop which we needed for the layout. The final board has a retaining wall climbing up to the height of the road bridge as the backdrop. This starts against the backscene board and spreads to be 70mm out when it reaches the main road bridge.

The retaining wall and road bridge piers are cut from mounting card which has been layered together for strength. The road itself is 3mm MDF supported by blocks of 69mm x 18mm timber.

The brickwork on the retaining wall and road bridge is from the Redutex range – this time using its engineering brick sheets for a change in colour. Evergreen plastic sheet and strip has then been used to detail the walling, adding in lintels and capping which have been painted with Humbrol No. 165.

With all the buildings built and in place a couple

WHAT WE USED		
Product	Manufacturer/Supplier	Cat No.
Champion Packing Plant	Walthers/Gaugemaster	3048
Weathering brick 3D texture sheets	Redutex	076LD122
Plain bond brick 3D texture sheets	Redutex	076LD112
Engineering brick 3D texture sheets	Redutex	076LD814
Department store	Metcalfe	PO279
Foamboard	Hobbycraft	
Mounting card	Hobbycraft	
Worn Brick acrylic	Lifecolor	UA737
Old Tile acrylic	Lifecolor	UA740
Rainmarks acrylic wash	Lifecolor	LPW11
BR Freight Grey acrylic	Lifecolor	UA818
Burned Black acrylic	Lifecolor	UA736
Brown acrylic aerosol	Humbrol	No. 29
Benches	Noch/Gaugemaster	14849
Ground cover	Greenscene	Various
Fine blended grey ballast	Woodland Scenics	B1393

A 'Warship' enters Platform 3 from the down fast with a uniform rake of BR maroon Mk 1s. The low relief retaining wall behind the stabling point is made from Redutex textured sheets over mounting card. Printed backscene elements may be added in this area in the future to increase the perceived 'depth' of the model.

of finishing touches were needed. First, a wall was needed to separate the railway from the factory sites and this was made from Redutex brick texture sheets mounted on thick card. Another point, which became obvious after painting the backscenes sky blue, was that the sky colour showed through the main factory building windows – a feature which didn't look quite right. Changing this was simple – the size of the buildings were marked on the

The 'Packing Plant' has been turned into a trio of substantial buildings which fill almost all of a 4ft long baseboard's backdrop.

A close up of the retaining wall behind the stabling point. Evergreen plastic strip has been added to detail the walls which are now ready for weathering.

backscene in pencil and grey paint was then used to fill the areas to make the interior of the factory buildings darker.

Building up the low relief buildings for Grosvenor Square has been a long part of the layout's development, but the variety of materials, sizes and styles of structure have made the backdrop to the railway interesting and varied enhancing the scene greatly. We hope you agree. ■

Developing the backdrop

Grosvenor Square needed a busy backdrop to suit its city location. With 12ft of space to fill that was a lot to achieve.

A first mock-up of the much modified Walthers Champion Packing Plant.

The full length of the modified Packing Plant factory building fills nearly all of a 4ft baseboard on its own.

for Grosvenor Square

Foamboard mock ups for the next factory and the raised parkland give an idea of how it will look in the future.

The mock-up of the factory end was wrapped in Redutex weathered brick textured sheets to become the final building. Walling has been added using mounting card and another texture sheet from Redutex.

A narrow roof has been added to the three-bay factory using Redutex weathered wrought iron panelling.

To stop the sky blue colour showing through the main factory windows, the backscene was painted grey behind the buildings.

The city parkland is detailed with sea moss trees, Model Tree Shop hedgerows at each end and MiniNatur bushes along the leading edge to help provxide boundaries.

10 TOP TIPS STATION DETAILING

There are many ways to bring life to a station scene. **MIKE WILD** offers
10 top tips to make your layout's signature location stand out from the crowd

LAMPS

1 Choosing the right lamps can make a huge difference to the look of a station scene. Our first choice is DCC Concepts' working lamps with Grosvenor Square using its Great Western Railway coloured gas lamps. The manufacturer's range includes swan neck and oil lamps too, all available in a variety of regional colours. If these are too much for your budget, then Gaugemaster supplies a similar range while there also station lamps available from manufacturers including Train Save, Wickness Models and Layouts4U. If you are looking for non-operational lamps, the world is your oyster with Hornby, Bachmann, Peco and many others producing designs to suit different periods and tastes.

● **Visit *www.dccconcepts.com* or *www.gaugemaster.com* for more information.**

BENCHES

2 A bench might seem to be a standard fixture, and Hornby's platform bench in its Skaledale range can be used with a fresh coat of paint to populate almost any platform. For this project we turned to the impressive range of white metal products by Dart Castings to allow us to accurately model GWR 14ft benches. Each comes as a kit of four parts which have to be assembled with superglue. We then painted them with Humbrol Brick Red (No. 70) to match the colour of the platform canopy bases.

● **Visit *www.dartcastings.co.uk* for more information.**

TROLLEYS

3 Every station can benefit from a selection of platform trolleys and sack barrows and there are many types available ranging from rickety wooden designs through to the standard BRUTE trolleys which appeared in the 1960s. This station scene benefits from a complement of trolleys and barrows which have been raided from our bits box. The origins include Dart Castings, Merit and Hornby and they really look the part once they are loaded up.

● **Visit *www.dartcastings.co.uk* or *www.hornby.com* for more information.**

SIGNAGE

4 Period signage and platform numbers help to set the region and period theme of a station. Here we've used a selection of signage including items from the Trackside Signs self-adhesive range for speed of application. To give the platform numbers a dual purpose they have been positioned alongside the location of the magnets under the train shed to assist operators in knowing where to uncouple locomotives. Completing the signage theme are 'Way Out' signs from the same range and period adverts from a number of sources including Sankey Scenics around the station.

● Visit *www.tracksidedesigns.co.uk* and *www.sankeyscenics.co.uk* for more information.

BICYCLES

5 A couple of bicycles propped up against a fence can fill in a small area of otherwise empty space. A simple and effective touch. This pair is from Artitec supplied in the UK by John Ayrey Diecast.

● Visit *www.ayrey.co.uk* for more information.

FENCING

8 The impeccable Ratio range provides the source for this finely detailed plastic spear fencing that has been a signature of several *Hornby Magazine* station layouts. Simple to work with and suitable for a wide range of applications, it breathes life and detail into a station, marking the boundary between railway and public land. We've used a combination of straight sections and gates to create the fencing around our station including sections around the platform ends.

● Visit *www.peco-uk.com* for more information.

BUFFER STOPS

9 There are many different types of buffer stop which you might find at a railway station, but for a terminus like this one sizeable hydraulic buffers were the only option. Assembled from Peco kits, they feature sprung buffers and go together quickly and simply with only painting left to do to finish them off. In lesser used sidings or bay platforms tradition rail-built buffer stops would do the job.

● Visit *www.peco-uk.com* for more information.

PARCELS AND LUGGAGE

10 Luggage, mail bags, parcels, newspaper stacks, milk churns and baskets all help to add to a station scene and they can be positioned in many different locations too. Most would be collected around the area of the brake coach for loading (or after unloading), while others might be stacked outside a parcels office waiting for the arrival of the next train. The majority of the items on Grosvenor Square are from the Dart Castings range with milk churns and wicker baskets coming from the Hornby Skaledale collection. The Dart Castings items are supplied unpainted in white metal, but with a little time and careful paint colour selection they are simple to bring up to standard.

● Visit *www.dartcastings.co.uk* or *www.hornby.com* for more information.

NEWSPAPER STAND

6 It might be a basic kit, but this Peco newspaper stand has really helped to add to the look of the platform ends at Grosvenor Square. Finished with a couple of coats of Lifecolor wood colours and paper magazines and newspapers from the kit, it doesn't look bad at all and proves that even a simple kit like this has a place on a detailed model railway.

● Visit *www.peco-uk.com* for more information.

PEOPLE

7 People are vital to a station scene, but too many can be just as bad as not enough. We've only just begun populating Grosvenor Square with passengers and station staff, but we'll be adding to it in the future. Figures so far include white metal castings from Dart Castings together with passengers from the Bachmann Scenecraft range. More are needed, but it is a start.

● Visit *www.dartcastings.co.uk* and *www.bachmann.co.uk* for more information.

MIXED goods

Goods trains came in all sorts of shapes and sizes. **MARK CHIVERS** creates 25 mixed goods formations from real trains for 'OO' gauge using readily available rolling stock.

FOR SHEER VARIETY, MIXED goods train formations have to be amongst the most exciting to have operated on Britain's railway network. By their very nature, they carried a diverse range of products from perishable foods to domestic coal, livestock, timber, fuel oil and more, utilising a wide selection of rolling stock in the process. Not only that, the go-anywhere nature of mixed freight services meant that 'foreign' wagons could appear virtually anywhere on the network.

Small volumes of goods would be loaded into vans or open wagons, depending on the commodity carried. Some goods might require ventilation, while others would not and appropriate rolling stock was provided to cater for these needs. Insulated and refrigerated vans were also used for transporting more perishable produce, while open wagons were ideal for conveying timber and minerals.

A selection of specialist vehicles was also built including containers for small loads such as refrigerated/frozen foods or furniture while bogie bolster wagons were used to convey larger items such as steel girders or automotive parts. One-plank

'Lowfit' and 'Lowmac' wagons could carry tractors or road vehicles while larger bogie well wagons were ideal for conveying out of gauge items such as generators or boilers.

The diverse nature of the goods being carried would define the appearance of each mixed goods train formation and inevitably meant that no two days would be quite the same. Trains would usually be formed into specific services at major goods or marshalling yards from wagons received off other freight arrivals, such as trip freights and pick-up goods from small branch lines, as well as other freight services for onward transportation. Whilst mixed freight services played an important role on the railway, they were also costly in terms of manpower and infrastructure, often costing more to operate than they made in revenue.

Motive power

For modellers, suitable 'OO' gauge motive power is available from the main manufacturers ranging from small locomotives such as Hornby's Worsdell 'J15' 0-6-0 to freight stalwarts such as Bachmann's War Department (WD) 'Austerity' 2-8-0 and BR '9F' 2-10-0. Hornby's roster also includes a good selection

of suitable prototypes ranging from Churchward '2800' 2-8-0s to Stanier 'Black Five' 4-6-0s and Bulleid 'West Country' and 'Battle of Britain' 4-6-2s. Diesel modellers are spoilt for choice too, with newcomer Sutton's Locomotive Works' 'OO' gauge Class 24 Bo-Bo diesel being one of the most recent standout releases.

However, it is the variety of the wagon roster which really makes mixed goods trains stand out from the crowd and, again, the manufacturers have many of the signature vehicle types covered.

Bachmann's prolific range of 'OO' freight vehicles includes an excellent selection of 12ton ventilated/non-ventilated vans of varied heritage as well as BR-built examples.

More specialised vehicles such as insulated/refrigerated meat and fish vans, fruit vans and more are also covered. Tank wagons are also important with Bachmann's 14ton, 20ton anchor-mounted and 45ton TTA examples all suitable for use within mixed goods formations.

Dapol's 'OO' range also features regional 12ton box vans and 16ton steel mineral open wagons, but also plugs a few gaps with its 20ton steel mineral open wagons, nine-plank open wagons, six-wheel milk

tankers, salt vans and even BR gunpowder vans.

Hornby's 'OO' gauge range also includes a useful selection of wooden-bodied open wagons encompassing triple packs of five-plank open wagons, 20ton nine-plank open mineral wagons, 6-wheel milk tank wagons, 12ton box vans and super-detailed models of the BR 20ton coal hopper wagons, LMS horseboxes and ubiquitous BR 20ton brake vans.

New models currently under development include Southern Railway Bulleid and Maunsell-designed 10ton cattle wagons from Hornby while Oxford Rail is also quickly building its roster of suitable wooden-bodied open wagons for 'OO' too.

Forming the trains

Whilst not exhaustive, the following selection of mixed goods train formations aims to show the variety of vehicles used within these services through the years. Whilst many of the formations appear quite long, you can shorten or lengthen them according to the size you can accommodate on your layout - and bear in mind that these formations could change from one day to the next. Happy marshalling! ■

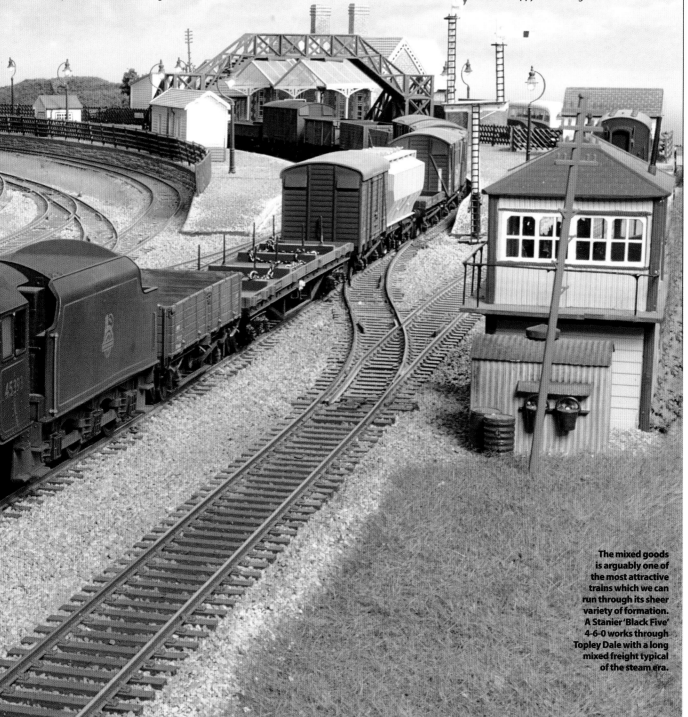

The mixed goods is arguably one of the most attractive trains which we can run through its sheer variety of formation. A Stanier 'Black Five' 4-6-0 works through Topley Dale with a long mixed freight typical of the steam era.

Maunsell 'S15' 4-6-0 BR black, early crests (Hornby), eight assorted BR 8ton/12ton cattle wagons, three BR 12ton vent vans, eight-plank open wagon*, BR 12ton plywood vent van, BR 12ton vent van, eight -plank open wagon*, three seven-plank open wagons*, SR 12ton vent van, three 14ton tank wagons, 16ton steel mineral open wagon*, two SR 12ton vent vans, three 16ton steel mineral open wagons*, BR 20ton brake van* – BR bauxite except *BR grey

Stanier 'Black Five' 4-6-0 BR black, early crests (Hornby), 8ton cattle wagon, BR 12ton plywood vent van, BR 12ton vent van, BR 12ton plywood vent van, BR 12ton vent van, 13ton high-sided steel open wagon, four 14ton tank wagons, 16ton steel mineral open wagon*, 14ton tank wagon, 16ton steel mineral open wagon*, three BR 12ton vent vans, four 16ton steel mineral open wagons, BR 20ton brake van – BR bauxite except *BR grey

Bulleid air-smoothed 'Battle of Britain' 4-6-2 BR lined green, early crests (Hornby), four 12ton planked vent vans, Conflat wagon + BD container, 16ton steel mineral open wagon**, 24ton Covhop wagon**, two 12ton planked vent vans, BR 20ton brake van, three 12ton planked vent vans, BR 20ton brake van, two 12ton planked vent vans, three 30ton bogie bolster wagons**, BR 20ton brake van – BR bauxite except **BR grey

Collett '2884' 2-8-0 BR black, late crests (Hornby), SR 12ton vent van, 13ton high-sided steel open wagon, three BR 12ton vent vans, 16ton steel mineral open wagon*, four 12ton vent vans, five 16ton steel mineral open wagons*, six 21ton grain hopper wagons*, BR 20ton brake van – BR bauxite except *BR grey

Adams 'O2' 0-4-4T BR lined black, late crests (Kernow), SR 'Pillbox' 25ton brake van*, four one-plank Lowfit wagons, SR 12ton vent van, BR 10ton insulated van**, BR 12ton vent van, Four Conflats + AF containers, BR 20ton brake van* – BR bauxite except *BR grey, **BR white
DATE: 1961 **SERVICE:** Trip freight **LOCATION:** Devonport

Peppercorn 'K1' 2-6-0 BR lined black, late crests (Hornby), BR Mk 1 CCT*, 12ton plywood vent van, two 12ton planked vent vans, two 16ton steel mineral open wagons**, 12ton plywood vent van, two 12ton planked vent vans, 12ton plywood vent van, two 12ton planked vent vans, five-plank open wagon**, seven-plank open wagon**, 12ton planked vent van, 12ton plywood vent van, Midland 20ton brake van – BR bauxite except **BR grey, *BR maroon

Fowler '4F' 0-6-0 BR black, late crests (Bachmann/Hornby), BR 12ton vent van, LMS 12ton vent van, two six-wheel milk tanks, LMS 12ton vent van, two 16ton steel mineral open wagons**, five-plank open wagon, Midland 20ton brake van** – BR bauxite except **BR grey
DATE: 1962 **SERVICE:** Carlisle to West Cumberland **LOCATION:** Cummersdale

'WD' 2-8-0 BR black, late crests (Bachmann), LMS 12ton vent van, BR 12ton plywood vent van, LMS 12ton vent van, BR 12ton vent van, 16ton steel mineral open wagon**, six 30ton bogie bolster wagons**, Midland 20ton brake van** - BR bauxite except **BR grey
DATE: 1963 **SERVICE:** Kingmoor to Skipton **LOCATION:** Cumwhinton

Stanier 'Jubilee' 4-6-0 BR lined green, late crests (Bachmann), six 30ton bogie bolster wagons, Conflat wagon + BD container*, four 16ton steel mineral open wagons, seven-plank open wagon, 30ton bogie bolster wagon, seven-plank open wagon, Midland 20ton brake van – BR grey except *BR bauxite

BR Class 22 BR green (Dapol), LNER 12ton vent van, 13ton steel 'Sand' tippler wagon, BR 12ton vent van, BR 12ton plywood vent van, GWR 20ton 'Toad' brake van - BR bauxite except
DATE: 1963 **SERVICE:** Kingsbridge to Hackney **LOCATION:** Brent

LMS rebuilt 'Royal Scot' 4-6-0 BR lined green, late crests (Hornby), BR 12ton vent van, two Conflats + AF containers, two 13ton high-sided steel open wagons, Conflat + BD container, five-plank open wagon, three BR 12ton vent vans, BR 10ton insulated van*, ten BR 12ton vent vans, two Conflats + BD containers, one BR 12ton vent vans, two 13ton high-sided steel open wagons, one 30ton bogie bolster wagons, Midland 20ton brake van**, LMS Fairburn 2-6-4T BR lined black, late crests (Bachmann) – BR bauxite except *BR white ** BR grey **DATE:** 1963 **SERVICE:** Oxley to Carlisle **LOCATION:** Oxenholme

Class 27 BR green, small yellow panels (Heljan), SR bogie B van*, BR 12ton plywood vent van, 13ton high-sided steel open wagon, five 22ton Presflo wagons, BR 20ton brake van – BR bauxite except *BR green **DATE:** 1963 **SERVICE:** Ballachulish to Connel Ferry **LOCATION:** Kentallen

DATE: 1956 SERVICE: Southbound freight LOCATION: Ash

DATE: 1957 SERVICE: Northbound freight LOCATION: Kingswood

DATE: 1958 SERVICE: Down Freight LOCATION: Yeovil Junction

DATE: 1959 SERVICE: Bristol to Tavistock Junction LOCATION: Dawlish

DATE: 1961 SERVICE: Mallaig to Fort William LOCATION: Fort William

'OO' FREIGHT ROLLING STOCK			
Type	**Livery**	**Manufacturer**	**Cat No.**
8ton/12ton GWR/BR cattle wagon	BR bauxite	Bachmann	37-712C
BR 10ton insulated van	BR ice blue	Bachmann	38-190A
BR 10ton insulated van	BR white	Bachmann	38-191B
BR 12ton fruit van	BR bauxite	Bachmann	38-183
BR 12ton pipe wagon	BR bauxite	Bachmann	38-701
BR 12ton shock absorbing van	BR bauxite	Bachmann	37-903A
BR 12ton vent van corrugated ends	BR bauxite	Bachmann	38-171C
BR 12ton vent van planked ends	BR bauxite	Bachmann	38-161B
BR 12ton vent van plywood ends	BR bauxite	Bachmann	38-170C
BR 12ton vent van (triple pack)	BR bauxite	Hornby	R6713
BR 20ton brake van	BR bauxite	Bachmann	37-530
BR 20ton brake van	BR bauxite	Hornby	R6508
BR 20ton brake van	BR grey	Bachmann	37-528C
BR 20ton coal hopper wagon	BR grey	Hornby	R6677
BR 21ton grain hopper wagons	BR grey	Bachmann	38-600A
BR 22ton tube wagon	BR bauxite	Bachmann	38-752
BR 24ton Covhop hopper wagon	BR grey	Bachmann	38-501A
BR 'Lowmac' wagon	BR bauxite	Hornby	R6399
BR Mk 1 Covered Carriage Truck (CCT)	BR maroon	Invicta	39-550Z
GWR 12ton fruit van	BR bauxite	Bachmann	37-754D
GWR 12ton Mogo van	BR bauxite	Bachmann	37-780
GWR 12ton shock absorbing van	BR bauxite	Bachmann	37-902A
GWR 12ton vent van	BR bauxite	Bachmann	37-729B
GWR 20ton 'Toad' brake van	BR grey	Bachmann	33-306C
GWR 20ton 'Toad' brake van	BR grey	Hornby	R6694
GWR 20ton 'Toad' brake van	BR bauxite	Bachmann	33-307
SR 12ton vent van 2+2 planks	BR bauxite	Bachmann	38-082C
SR 12ton vent van plywood	BR bauxite	Bachmann	38-076C
SR 25ton 'Pill box' brake van	BR bauxite	Bachmann	38-402
SR 25ton 'Pill box' brake van	BR grey	Bachmann	38-401
SR bogie Van B	BR blue	Hornby	R4585
LMS 12ton vent van	BR bauxite	Bachmann	37-802C
LMS 20ton brake van	BR grey	Bachmann	38-550
LMS Horsebox	BR crimson	Hornby	R6679A
LNER 12ton fish van	BR bauxite	Bachmann	38-577
LNER 12ton fruit van	BR bauxite	Bachmann	38-385A
LNER 12ton vent van corr. ends	BR bauxite	Bachmann	38-381
LNER 12ton vent van planked ends	BR bauxite	Bachmann	38-376
LNER 12ton non-vent van	BR bauxite	Bachmann	38-476
LNER Gresley 61ft 6in Full Brake (BG)	BR maroon	Hornby	R4531C
12ton shock absorbing open wagon	BR bauxite	Bachmann	38-879
13ton high-sided steel open wagon	BR bauxite	Bachmann	38-326
14ton 'Mermaid' side tipping wagon	BR black	Flangeway	ME-10
14ton tank wagons (set of three)	Black	Bachmann	37-670A
16ton steel mineral open wagon	BR bauxite	Bachmann	37-256

DATE: 1963 SERVICE: Durranhill to Skipton LOCATION: Cotehill

Maunsell 'N' 2-6-0 BR lined black, late crests (Bachmann), GWR 12ton fruit van, BR 12ton plywood vent van, SR 12ton vent van, BR 16ton steel mineral open wagon*, two BR 12ton plywood vent vans, two 16ton steel mineral open wagons*, BR 12ton vent van, Midland 20ton brake van* - BR bauxite except *BR grey
DATE: 1963 SERVICE: Barnstaple Junction to Exmouth Junction LOCATION: Crediton

BR Standard '9F' 2-10-0 BR black, late crests (Bachmann/Hornby), 13ton high-sided steel open wagon, seven-plank open wagon*, 13ton high sided steel open wagon, two five-plank open wagons*, 15 Conflat wagons + AFU containers**, BR 20ton brake van – BR bauxite except *BR grey, **white

Class 24 BR green, small yellow panels (Bachmann/SLW), eight BR 12ton vent vans, 30ton bogie bolster wagon*, SR 12ton vent van, LNER 12ton fruit van, two 13ton high-sided steel open wagons, five 16ton steel mineral open wagons*, two 20ton anchor mounted tank wagons**, BR 20ton brake van – BR bauxite except *BR grey, **Esso black

Class 52 BR maroon, small yellow panels (Dapol/Heljan), SR 12ton vent van, LMS 12ton vent van, SR 12ton vent van, two BR 12ton vent vans, five-plank open wagon, one-plank 'Lowfit' wagon, seven-plank open wagon*, BR 12ton vent van, two Conflats + AF containers, SR 12ton vent van, two BR 12ton vent vans, SR 12ton vent van, three BR 12ton vent vans, eight 16ton steel mineral open wagons*, BR 20ton brake van – BR bauxite except *BR grey

Class 26 BR green, small yellow panels (Heljan), four BR 12ton plywood vent vans, 16ton steel mineral open wagon*, five-plank open wagon*, 16ton steel mineral open wagon*, BR 20ton brake van – BR bauxite except *BR grey   DATE: 1966   SERVICE: Crieff to Perth   LOCATION: Crieff

Stanier 'Black Five' 4-6-0 BR black, late crests (Hornby), BR 12ton plywood vent van, LMS 12ton vent van, BR 12ton shock absorbing van, SR 12ton vent van, five-plank open wagon, BR 12ton plywood vent van, LMS 12ton vent van, BR 12ton vent van, 12ton pipe wagon, Conflat wagon + BD container, 12ton pipe wagon, two Conflat wagons + BD container, 16ton steel mineral open wagon**, 30ton bogie bolster wagon**, 13ton high-sided steel open wagon, 20ton coal hopper**, 30ton bogie bolster wagon**, BR 20ton brake van – BR bauxite except **BR grey

BR '4MT' 4-6-0 BR lined black, late crests (Bachmann/Hornby), 45ton TTA tank wagon (Shell/BP)**, two 13ton high-sided steel open wagon, 16ton steel mineral open wagon**, BR 20ton brake van – BR bauxite except **BR grey   DATE: 1968   SERVICE: Unidentified   LOCATION: Arnside

Class 42 BR blue (Bachmann), 15 BR 12ton vent vans, Conflat + BD container, two BR 12ton plywood vent vans, eight 16ton steel mineral open wagons**, BR 'Grampus' ballast wagon*, BR 20ton brake van – BR bauxite except *BR black

Class 25/0 BR blue (Bachmann), two BR 12ton plywood vent vans, three 13ton high-sided steel open wagons, BR 12ton plywood vent van, three 16ton steel mineral open wagons*, 65ton Weltrol WH bogie well-wagon*, seven five-plank open wagons, three 16ton steel mineral open wagons*, BR 20ton brake van – BR bauxite except* BR grey

Class 24 BR blue (Bachmann/SLW), two BR 12ton plywood vent vans, 13ton high-sided steel open wagon, five 16ton steel mineral open wagons*, two BR 20ton coal hopper wagons*, three 16ton steel mineral open wagons*, 30ton bogie bolster wagon, BR 20ton brake van – BR bauxite except *BR grey

Class 40 BR blue (Bachmann), two 13ton high-sided steel open wagons, four 20ton 'Grampus' ballast wagons, three 16ton steel mineral open wagons*, 13ton high-si steel open wagon, two 16ton steel mineral open wagons*, BR 12ton vent van, 16ton steel mineral open wagon*, three BR 12ton vent vans, BR 20ton brake van – BR b except *BR grey

Class 37/0 BR blue (Bachmann/ViTrains), BR 12ton plywood vent van, five-plank open wagon, 80ton BDA bogie bolster wagon**, 20ton coal hopper wagon*, four 16ton steel mineral open wagons*, 80ton BDA bogie bolster wagon**, three 16ton steel mineral open wagons*, 20ton coal hopper wagon*, two 12ton vent vans, BR 20ton brake van – BR bauxite except *BR grey, **BR Railfreight red

Class 27 BR blue (Heljan), 13ton high-sided steel open wagon*, three 16ton steel mineral open wagons, BR 24ton Covhop wagon*, 16ton steel mineral wagon, five BR 24ton Covhop wagons*, BR 20ton brake van* – BR grey except *BR bauxite   DATE: 1979   SERVICE: Cadder Yard to Fort William   LOCATION: Ardlui

DATE: 1965 SERVICE: Southbound freight LOCATION: Crossmyloof

DATE: 1965 SERVICE: Northbound freight LOCATION: Dava

DATE: 1965 SERVICE: Westbound mixed freight LOCATION: Taunton

DATE: 1967 SERVICE: Southbound mixed freight LOCATION: Dent

DATE: 1971 SERVICE: Eastbound mixed freight LOCATION: Plymouth

DATE: 1972 SERVICE: Down mixed freight LOCATION: Coaltown of Balgonie

DATE: 1975 SERVICE: Warrington Arpley freight LOCATION: Thelwall

DATE: 1979 SERVICE: Warrington freight LOCATION: Skelton Junction

DATE: 1979 SERVICE: Healey Mills freight LOCATION: Horbury

'OO' FREIGHT ROLLING STOCK			
Type	Livery	Manufacturer	Cat No.
16ton steel mineral open wagon	BR bauxite	Bachmann	37-226F
16ton steel mineral open – top flap	BR grey	Bachmann	37-225G
16ton steel mineral open no top flap	BR grey	Bachmann	37-250H
16ton steel mineral open pressed end	BR grey	Bachmann	37-378
20ton anchor-mounted tank	Shell/BP black	Bachmann	38-776
20ton anchor-mounted tank	Esso black	Bachmann	38-777
20ton 'Grampus' ballast wagon	BR black	Dapol	4F-060-008
22ton 'Presflo' wagon (triple pack)	BR bauxite	Bachmann	38-287
30ton bogie bolster wagon	BR grey	Bachmann	33-856D
31ton OBA open wagon	BR Railfreight	Bachmann	38-041B

31ton OCA dropside open wagon	BR Railfreight	Bachmann	38-056A
45ton TTA tank wagon	Shell/BP grey	Bachmann	37-577A
45ton VBA sliding door van	BR bauxite	Bachmann	38-126A
45ton VDA sliding door van	BR Railfreight	Bachmann	38-140
46ton HEA hopper wagon	BR Railfreight	Bachmann	38-006D
46ton VGA sliding wall van	BR Railfreight	Bachmann	37-601A
65ton 'Weltrol WH' bogie well-wagon	BR grey	Bachmann	33-901E
80ton BDA bogie bolster wagon	BR Railfreight	Bachmann	38-151B
Conflat wagon with A container	BR bauxite	Bachmann	37-961
Conflat wagon with AF containers	BR bauxite	Bachmann	37-981
Conflat with BD container	BR bauxite	Bachmann	37-951B
Six-wheel milk tank	Co-op white	Dapol	B654
One-plank 'Lowfit' wagon	BR bauxite	Bachmann	37-479
Three-plank open wagon	BR bauxite	Bachmann	37-930
Five-plank open wagon	BR grey	Bachmann	37-016C
Five-plank open wagon (triple pack)	BR bauxite	Bachmann	R6712
Six-plank open wagon	BR grey	Oxford Rail	OR76MW4002
Seven-plank open wagon	BR grey	Bachmann	37-081F
Seven-plank open wagon	BR grey	Oxford Rail	OR76MW7013
Eight-plank open wagon	BR grey	Bachmann	37-158C
Nine-plank open mineral wagon	BR grey	Dapol	4F-090-005
Nine-plank open mineral wagon	BR grey	Hornby	R6108G

USEFUL LINKS	
Bachmann	www.bachmann.co.uk
Dapol	www.dapol.co.uk
Flangeway	www.flangeway.com
Heljan	www.heljan.dk
Hornby	www.hornby.com
Invicta Model Rail	www.invictamodelrail.com
Kernow Model Rail Centre	www.kernowmodelrailcentre.com
Oxford Rail	www.oxfordrail.com
Suttons Loco Workshop (SLW)	www.sulzertype2.co.uk
ViTrains	www.vitrains.it

A roof over our heads

Hornby Magazine's roofing contractor **TIM SHACKLETON** describes the construction of Grosvenor Square's imposing overall canopy.

I WANTED PEOPLE TO LOOK at this model and think 'That looks impressive' rather than 'That's a Peco station roof'. It's built on a larger scale than many people would attempt, but at heart it's still the same plastic kit you can buy at your local model shop – only with more of them!

Considering the amount of time I had available – basically, a Bank Holiday weekend with a few hours either side – building a roof this size using anything other than a simple kit was out of the question and Peco's well-regarded plastic model was the obvious choice. Had I had time – an awful lot of time – I might have considered the astonishing Alan Gibson etched brass kit of Bath Green Park's canopy but with a deadline measured in days rather than months it was obvious that practicality, as ever, would hold sway.

For the most part the kits are built exactly

as supplied but I made extensive use of pre-painting techniques I've picked up over the years to differentiate the completed model from many hundreds exactly like it. One governing factor was the observation that real station roofs on this kind of scale – I was thinking particularly of places I once knew such as Manchester Central, Bradford Exchange and Broad Street – have a delicate, almost spidery appearance. The glazing, though heavily discoloured, will exhibit any number of subtle 'glass' tones that are barely distinguishable from each other, as well as large numbers of replacement panes.

For ease of assembly the Peco kit is pretty robust and the glazing is quite chunky. You can play this down with careful painting in light colours, accentuated by subtle weathering effects.

Each kit contains 170 separate components which can be combined to make two complete bay units and altogether I used three full kits to assemble the roof, plus an additional scratchbuilt section making just shy of seven bays in all. There is a lot of repetition involved so patience is a virtue!

I built the roofs systematically on what amounted to an industrial production line – **Step 1** paint all glazing; **Step 2** paint all columns; **Step 3** paint all trusses; **Step 4** assemble glazing and trusses as one unit; **Step 5** wash over glazing; **Step 6** add columns and **Step 7** fit the whole lot together. Guess which stage took longest?

Grosvenor Square's station canopy in all its glory, during a trial installation. I wanted to suggest the down-at-heel decrepitude of a less image-conscious era, when appearances mattered less than simply keeping the trains running.

TOOLS

» Craft knife
» Stanley knife
» Sprue cutters
» Xuron side cutters
» Emery boards
» Plastic cutter
» Paint brushes
» Humbrol Liquid Poly

PLEASE TURN FOR STEP BY STEP GUIDE

CONSTRUCTION

STEP BY STEP **BUILDING PECO OVERALL ROOF**

SKILL LEVEL Beginner — Intermediate — Advanced

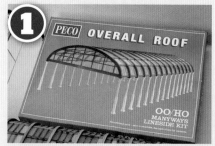

1 Beginning and end – the Peco roof kit has long been a staple of the UK modelling scene, protecting 4mm scale passengers from the elements for many years. With a bit of creativity it offers more scope than you might imagine.

2 I'm fascinated by aerial photography, so despite the tight schedule I found time to plough through some of my books on the subject in search of inspiration about what railway stations and other glass-roofed structures look like from the air.

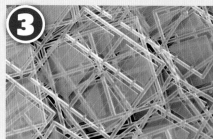

3 Station roof glazing that's been exposed for years to smoke, steam and the elements doesn't gleam like plate glass. The first step was to kill the shine on the clear plastic mouldings with a couple of coats of Testor's Dullcote.

4 I then painted random panes with very pale grey – a mixture of Lifecolor UA603 Hellgrau and UA708 Light Dust. Reflecting the differences between replacement panes fitted over the years, this gives a characteristic variety between clear and opaque.

5 The roof ribs were airbrushed light grey (Lifecolour UA603 Hellgrau again) to represent the metallic grey paint so often seen on such structures. In 4mm scale you don't need any metallic sparkle.

6 I allowed the paint to dry overnight and then began assembling the components – close to 600 parts in total. The first stage was to get the trusses and girders assembled, using the glazing to brace it. This is the critical phase – once you get everything square, true and solidly seated, the rest is plain sailing. Humbrol Liquid Poly was used to secure everything together.

7 Carry on adding trusses and glazing sections until each roof unit is finished. Slotting components over a framework of rods is very much on the same principles as a child's construction toy – my generation will register the similarities with Bayko!

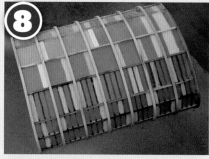

8 This is what we end up with – just five more of these sections to go! The glazing panels have been added entirely randomly to create a prototypical appearance.

9 The detail of the roof is quite understated but it really starts to come to life when you run a thin dark wash along the glazing bars. I used a couple of enamel colours, Revell Charcoal (9) warmed up with a hint of Humbrol Matt Leather (62) and diluted with a 60% infusion of white spirit. By comparing the results with the untouched panel on the left, you can see it makes quite a difference. Getting the glazing to look the part took longer than the rest of the painting/assembly process put together!

10 I wanted the bases of the canopy support columns to be a Western Region colour, dulled down over the years. I settled on Humbrol Brick Red (No 70) for its flat chocolate tone – not at all the deep lustrous shade of GWR carriages. By the early 1960s this had a tired, last-legs look that would soon be swept away by BR's brand-new corporate identity.

11 I assembled the columns in one hit. Only the bases are painted, the rest is the natural colour of the plastic. I think it's perhaps a little too intense for WR cream but I wanted to emphasise the regional colours and make it visible from a distance.

12 The canopy supports are cut from their sprues and cleaned up as necessary. Remember to file the bases smooth, otherwise they won't sit properly.

13 I made the end cladding from a sheet of 20thou styrene, scored to represent planking. One panel has been removed to suggest material deterioration and neglect.

14 Once the roof is completed your main problem is keeping the different sections aligned. On a permanent layout, they can be glued or preferably bolted together. On a portable exhibition layout such as Grosvenor Square this largely has to be done by eye, a nudge here and a tweak there.

15 The roof units ride piggyback on each other, using simple 'shelves' made from 2mm Plastruct sheet. The second line of roof sections has supports only on the visible side.

Inspiration for the cut-down roof at one end of the station came from this shot of Fairburn 2-6-4T 42233 leaving Huddersfield in April 1967 with the three-coach 9.14am train to King's Cross. At Wakefield Westgate it would combine with the main portion from Leeds.

Creating the part-dismantled section at one end added individuality and was a good way of using up spare components such as roof braces and glazing panels. I made the extra girders I needed out of Evergreen styrene section cut to length using the guillotine-like Chopper from US company North West Short Line.

Once the components had been assembled (Evergreen styrene responds brilliantly to Humbrol Liquid Poly) I brush-painted the framework with LifeColour Hellgrau. The extra bracing – which is there purely for appearance – is Alan Gibson's 0.9mm hard brass wire.

I cut up spare glazing sections using a circular saw in a mini-drill, then slotted them in place. At this stage the end roof section stands on temporary legs for support.

The Peco kit is transformed by the sawn-off canopy and the makeshift end cover, which looks as if it could have been there for decades.

TIP

Painting components before assembly can make a project simpler to complete. We used this method throughout the canopy construction for Grosvenor Square.

WHAT WE USED		
Overall roof plastic kit	Peco	LK-20X
2mm plastic sheet	Evergreen	9080
4mm 'I' section plastic section	Evergreen	275
0.9mm brass wire	Alan Gibson	4M137
Dullcote	Testors	1260
Hellgrau	Lifecolor	UA603
Light Dust	Lifecolor	UA708
Charcoal	Revell	9
Matt Leather	Humbrol	62
Brick Red	Humbrol	70

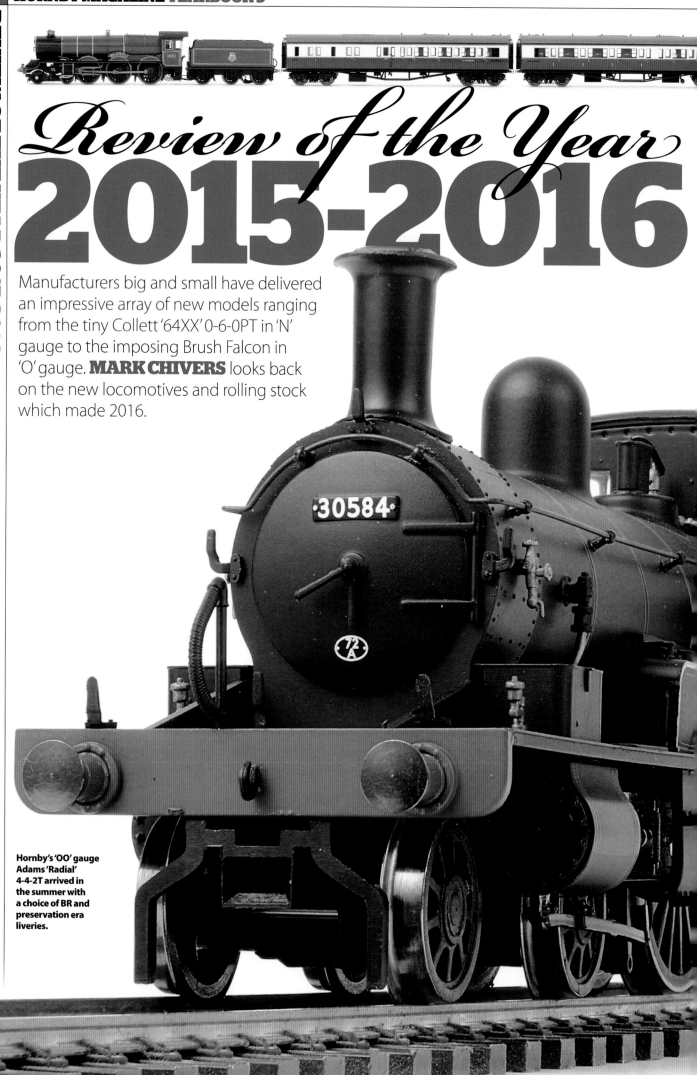

Review of the Year
2015-2016

Manufacturers big and small have delivered an impressive array of new models ranging from the tiny Collett '64XX' 0-6-0PT in 'N' gauge to the imposing Brush Falcon in 'O' gauge. **MARK CHIVERS** looks back on the new locomotives and rolling stock which made 2016.

Hornby's 'OO' gauge Adams 'Radial' 4-4-2T arrived in the summer with a choice of BR and preservation era liveries.

Hornby released a selection of Collett bow-end carriages for 'OO' with a choice of BR carmine and cream and GWR chocolate and cream colour schemes.

2016 HAS CERTAINLY BEEN a roller-coaster year for the hobby, with its fair share of highs and lows including high-profile financial issues and some significant price rises. All that aside, most importantly for us it has included some incredible new models along the way too.

Hornby has delivered an impressive stream of newly-tooled 'OO' models during the past 12 months including its London & South Western Railway (LSWR) Adams '0415' 4-4-2T, Class 71 Bo-Bo electric, London and North Eastern Railway (LNER) Raven 'Q6' 0-8-0 and two sets of carriages – Great Western Railway (GWR) 57ft Collett 'bow-end' vehicles and rebuilt LSWR Maunsell 58ft non-corridor stock.

Whilst development of Bachmann's 'OO' and 'N' gauge projects had slowed, the company announced that it had arranged for more

Minerva Model Railways delivered its debut model in this smart 'O' gauge model of the Peckett 'E' 0-4-0ST.

resources to be available to enable progress to accelerate on already-announced models. In October, as this book closed for press, it looks like Bachmann was starting to turn the corner with arrival of its Wickham Type 27 permanent way trolley and progress on its outstanding projects being shown in new engineering samples. Heljan has continued to develop its range of 'O' gauge models, with a number of significant arrivals while in 'OO' it made its first general release steam locomotive, the LNER Gresley 'O2' 2-8-0.

More recent entrants to the hobby also delivered well-received new products to market including DJ Models' 'OO' Hunslet 'Austerity' 0-6-0ST and Oxford Rail's 'OO' LSWR Adams '0415' 4-4-2T. However, there were two models in particular that made the headlines for the right reasons this year - Rapido Trains' exclusive venture with Locomotion Models which saw them deliver their first British-outline 'OO' gauge model in the stunning Advanced Passenger Train – Experimental and Rail Exclusive's Philip Sutton who launched his Sutton's Locomotive Workshops brand, which caught many off-guard, not just with the announcement and subsequent high specification for his new Class 24 Bo-Bo diesel, but the fact that it was also physically available for purchase on the day of the launch.

Britain's first fully crowd-funded 'N' gauge model was also delivered by the fledgling Revolution Trains (RT) with its Rapido Trains-produced VTG/Greenbrier TEA bogie tank wagons. With more

projects in the pipeline and its 'N' gauge ready-to-run Class 390 'Pendolino' Electric Multiple Unit due soon, there's much to look forward to.

And this is all just the tip of the iceberg - 2016 proved to be another impressive year for ready-to-run models.

October

The year's review begins with the arrival of Hornby's new 'OO' Maunsell 'S15' 4-6-0 with retailers – our exclusive first review appearing in HM100. Three models formed the initial batch as 30843 in BR black with early crests and straight-sided tender together with 30830 in BR black carrying late crests and 824 in Southern Railway (SR) olive green both coupled to standard bogie tenders with flared sides.

Meanwhile, Kernow Model Rail Centre received the first of its Isle of Wight 'O2' 0-4-4Ts with extended coal bunker, alternative smokebox door and four lamp bracket positions. Our sample was decorated as 24 *Calbourne*, the sole surviving example of the class which is located on the Isle of Wight Steam Railway.

November

Occasionally, a model arrives that truly takes your breath away. This was certainly the case when Sutton's Locomotive Workshops surprised the hobby with its unexpected and outstanding 'OO' gauge BR Sulzer Type 2. Setting a new benchmark for 'OO' gauge diesels, the specification called »

New for 'N' gauge from Bachmann's Graham Farish brand was the BR '4MT' 2-6-4T.

for incredible levels of detail, while digital sound versions were also offered with a twin-speaker arrangement and extensive suite of quality audio.

Oxford Rail released its debut ready-to-run steam locomotive in the month with the arrival of its first 'OO' LSWR Adams '0415' 4-4-2T. Given that two models of this locomotive type had been announced (the second in development with Hornby), much was riding on its arrival. Finished as 30583 in BR lined black with late crests, Oxford Rail's 'Radial' certainly looked the part with its fine rivet detail, full complement of lamp irons and sprung metal buffers.

For DCC sound users Hornby delivered the first of its 'OO' Collett 'King' 4-6-0s to feature Twin Track Sound (TTS), decorated as 6021 *King Richard II* in BR blue. Sound functions included four different

whistles, wheel slip, coal shovelling and more.

'O' gauge modellers weren't forgotten either as Heljan's impressive Brush Class 60 Co-Co diesel-electric touched down during the month, offering a stunning contemporary model. Three versions appeared in BR Railfreight triple grey, EWS maroon and gold and the distinctive Loadhaul black and orange, although there was a mistake with the angles of this latter livery on our review sample.

Heljan also delivered its ready-to-run 'O' gauge 19.5ton 'Catfish' and 24.5ton 'Dogfish' ballast hopper wagons with a choice of BR black, olive green and 'Dutch' grey and yellow liveries.

Finally, Key Publishing's 'OO' gauge Diesel Brake Tender arrived just in time for the 2015 Warley National Model Railway Exhibition at the NEC in Birmingham. Three versions were available from

the *Hornby Magazine* stand at the show – one in BR plain green and two in BR Green with small yellow panels. A fourth in BR blue subsequently arrived in October 2016.

December

Arriving just in time for Christmas was Dapol's 'OO' gauge Class 73. Whilst the development of this model had been somewhat protracted, first impressions were favourable, the model capturing the box-like appearance of the prototypes well.

Hornby's 'OO' gauge LNER Gresley 'J50' 0-6-0T also surfaced for review during the month, its long sloped front side tanks looking just so, including the distinctive cut-out above the leading drive wheels. Despite its diminutive size, the 'J50' handled eight coaches with ease and

A trio of Class 71s made up the debut collection from Hornby for this new 'OO' gauge mdoel.

demonstrated smooth and near silent control.

For 'O' gauge modellers, Minerva Models debuted its first 7mm scale locomotive - the Peckett 'E' class 0-4-0ST. Available in a selection of liveries, each was supplied with a set of etched brass worksplates, lamp irons, numberplates, an optional toolbox and a choice of three domes.

It's not every day that a contemporary model appears in close succession to the prototype, but that's exactly what happened when we received samples of Drax Power Station's exclusive 'OO' gauge biomass bogie wagons. Manufactured by Hornby, two wagons were produced, each carrying subtly different branding and intended as promotional items for Drax. A limited number of models were subsequently made available for modellers exclusively through Hatton's of Liverpool.

At the other end of the scale, Bachmann's 'N' gauge BR 12ton pipe wagons arrived too offering a new choice of steam era goods wagon.

January

Eastern Region motive power greeted 2016 with the release of Heljan's 'OO' gauge LNER Gresley 'O2/3' and 'O2/4' 2-8-0s. Weighing in at 510g, this model offered impressive haulage capacity with our tests seeing it loaded to 60 wagons.

With the increasing popularity of 'O' gauge, specialist manufacturer Lionheart Trains delivered its new ready-to-run Air Ministry 14ton tank wagons. Based on prototypes built between 1938 and 1942, Lionheart modelled both Class A and Class B versions, replicating the detail differences between both types. In total 16 different livery variations were produced by Lionheart.

Finally, Gaugemaster commissioned a colourful exclusive limited edition model of Dapol's 'OO' gauge Class 73 electro-diesel in Pullman colours. Decorated as 73101 in Pullman umber and cream, the model appeared in both *Brighton Evening Argus* and *The Royal Alex* guises. »

Dapol's Class 73 was released just before Christmas for 'OO'.

The GWR 'King' 4-6-0 from Hornby received a Twin Track Sound decoder in 2016.

Oxford Rail's first ready-to-run locomotive arrival was the Adams 'Radial' 4-4-2T.

Dapol's Class 33 for 'N' gauge.

February

Brush prototype diesel D0280 *Falcon* appeared in super-sized form during February with Heljan's 'O' gauge release of this imposing locomotive. Our review sample was decorated in BR two-tone green as carried while in BR ownership on the Western Region in the 1960s. Capturing the long slab-sided design to a tee, Heljan's powerful model featured twin operating roof fans, directional lighting and smooth performance.

Oxford Rail's second issue of its new 'OO' LSWR Adams Radial 4-4-2T emerged with 30584 in BR lined black with late crests. Following feedback to the manufacturer, this latest release featured revised tolerances for improved running characteristics, finer wheel flange depths and improvements to the fit of detail parts.

Given the recent influx of suitable GWR motive power, it was only natural that Hornby would introduce a new series of suitable 'OO' coaches, and during February its Collett 57ft 'bow-end' vehicles appeared. Five variants encompassing three vehicle types were delivered, with left and right handed Corridor Brake Third and Corridor Composites together with a single Corridor Third, each available in GWR chocolate and cream and BR carmine and cream.

With renewed interest in 'OO9' modelling following recent announcements from Bachmann and Heljan, Peco have also been developing new vehicles and added a trio of Glyn Valley Tramway vehicles to its range of ready-to-run models.

March

Rolling stock was very much the order of the day during March with Heljan's impressive 'O' gauge Cargowaggon IWB bogie vans and IGA flat bogie wagons trundling in to the *Hornby Magazine* office. Five vans and four flats formed the initial batch of models. From an earlier period, Lionheart Trains delivered its 'O' gauge 16ton mineral wagons which appeared as Diagram 1/108 welded and 1/109 riveted examples.

For modellers of the contemporary scene in 'OO', Dapol delighted with its new Freightliner HIA bogie limestone hoppers. Available in Freightliner green and Freightliner white liveries, they featured well-detailed die-cast metal wagon bodies on free running chassis which proved incredibly popular, the first runs selling through very quickly.

Hornby's TTS range was bolstered with the addition of its high-fidelity Class 67 diesel-electric. This was the first time one of the manufacturer's main range diesel locomotives had appeared factory-fitted with its cost-effective Digital

Command Control (DCC) sound decoder. Finished as 67004 *Cairn Gorm* in Caledonian Sleeper livery, the onboard decoder included 25 functions. It looked and sounded superb.

Perfect for an officer's special, Bachmann's London Midland and Scottish Railway (LMS) 50ft inspection saloon was officially added to the Graham Farish range for the first time. Previously only available to members of the N Gauge Society, it appeared in LMS lined maroon with black ends, BR lined maroon and BR blue and grey.

April

One of the standout models of the year has to be Locomotion Models' spectacular 'OO' gauge four-car Advanced Passenger Train – Experimental

(APT-E). Exclusive to the NRM National Collection in Miniature range, this specially commissioned model was produced by Rapido Trains and represented the Canadian manufacturer's first British outline ready-to-run 'OO' gauge model to bear its name.

Detail levels were exceptional with exquisite rivet detail, detailed interiors, illuminated interior equipment consoles and even different windscreen wiper arrangements at each end. Performance was smooth and consistent thanks to a heavy die-cast chassis and five-pole skew wound motor at each end while DCC sound-fitted versions featured realistic gas turbine sounds which really elevated this model - and it tilted too!

Bachmann's newly-tooled 'OO' gauge Southern

Heljan's 'O' gauge Class 60 showed the manufacturer's ability to produce striking locomotives in the larger scale.

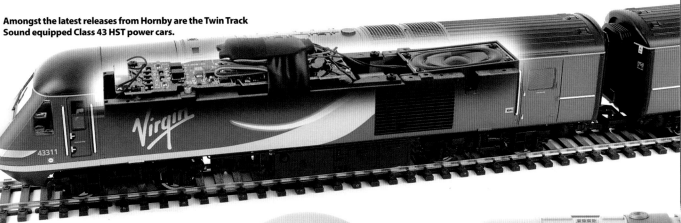

Amongst the latest releases from Hornby are the Twin Track Sound equipped Class 43 HST power cars.

Right: **Sutton's Locomotive Workshop's Sulzer Type 2 for 'OO'.**

Railway Passenger Luggage Vans and Covered Carriage Trucks also rolled in, replicating these widely travelled vehicles superbly in SR olive green, BR green and BR blue liveries. Meanwhile, Bachmann's 14ton and 20ton anchor-mounted 10ft wheelbase tankers for 'OO' also docked. Detail and finish was exemplary, just as we've come to expect from the manufacturer.

May

Another locomotive which has been the subject for two manufacturers is BR's Class 71 Bo-Bo electric. First to arrive for review was Hornby's 'OO' gauge model. Announced by the manufacturer in 2014 at the Warley National Model Railway Exhibition, the Class 71 is also the subject of a crowd-funded 'OO' model currently under development from DJ Models. Hornby's model certainly looked the part and ran exceptionally well. Available in BR green, BR green with small yellow panels and BR blue liveries it also featured »

Drax biomass wagons for 'OO' produced exclusively for Drax Power Station by Hornby.

Lionheat Trains' 'O' gauge Air Ministry 14ton tanker.

directional lights and a functional overhead pantograph.

Heljan's sublime 'O' gauge Type 4 'Warship' B-B diesel-hydraulic rolled in during the month adding to the manufacturer's growing range of 'O' gauge diesel locomotives. Five standard models together with six limited editions for Tower Models were amongst the arrivals, capturing the look and distinctive curves of the prototype well. Twin five-pole motors and flywheels ensured the model ran as well as it looked.

For 'N' gauge modellers, Bachmann issued its GWR Collett '64XX' 0-6-0PT with three versions added to its Graham Farish range in GWR green, BR lined green and BR black. Each featured fine wire handrails, fine rivet detail and excellent decoration throughout with smooth and quiet running characteristics thanks to Bachmann's coreless motor.

June

Hornby was a force to be reckoned with as summer approached, with a number of locomotive projects coming to fruition. Hot on the heels of its Class 71, Hornby's 'OO' gauge LSWR Adams '0415' 4-4-2T arrived for review during the month. Revealed in November 2014, three versions including 488 in as-preserved LSWR green, 30582 in BR black with late crests and 30584 in BR black with early crests formed the initial releases. With competition from Oxford Rail earlier in the year, Hornby's model was well received, with detail variations across all three models such as chimney styles, cab rear window shapes, safety valve types and pony wheel sizes.

Next, Hornby's magnificent LNER Raven 'Q6' 0-8-0 appeared on the horizon. Bearing in mind that this stunning North Eastern Region model

Heljan 'O' gauge Cargowaggon.

Freightliner HIA limestone hopper for 'OO' from Dapol.

had only been announced at the 2015 Warley National Model Railway Exhibition, it was nothing short of remarkable. Tooling options allow early and late detail differences between class members as well as two tender styles. Three models appeared initially as 3418 in LNER black, 63443 in BR black with early crests and 63429 in BR black with late crests.

New 'OO' projects from Bachmann were fewer this year, although its 'OO' Gresley 'V3' 2-6-2T returned to the range with an upgraded chassis which features a DCC decoder socket for the first time. This model also brought with it a new

type of decoder socket – the Next18 – advancing the simplicity of installing both a decoder and additional features such as lamps. Space has also been provided for DCC sound installations, including wire routing, representing another step forward from the manufacturer.

Dapol's long-awaited 'N' gauge Southern Railway 'Schools' 4-4-0 surfaced during the summer and demonstrated a sense of finesse with its wealth of rivet details, separately applied detail parts and factory-fitted etched metal nameplates.

Another 'N' gauge highlight was Bachmann's delightful BR '4MT' 2-6-4T which also touched down in June. Announced in the 2012/2013

'OO' gauge saw the arrival of Heljan's Gresley 'O2' 2-8-0.

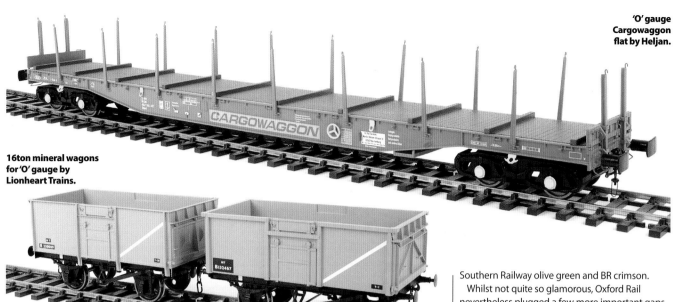

'O' gauge Cargowaggon flat by Heljan.

16ton mineral wagons for 'O' gauge by Lionheart Trains.

Graham Farish catalogue, the wait was certainly worthwhile as it bristled with detail throughout and running characteristics equalled its good looks with the manufacturer's coreless motor at its centre.

For those who missed out first time, Bachmann's 'OO' gauge Blue Pullman made a welcome return, this time with power cars M60092 and M60093 along with correctly numbered trailer cars. Decoration was exemplary as was the detailing inside and out, and this release was presented in a pack containing a reproduction menu card, fine art print, illustrated history of the train and a pack of 'OO' gauge stewards – an impressive package albeit at a not insignificant £599.95.

July

Bachmann's 'OO' gauge Ivatt '2MT' 2-6-2T benefitted from a new chassis too in 2016 which, like the 'V3', also had a Next18 decoder socket and provision for sound. Continuing the digital theme Bachmann achieved another first for the British market when it delivered its first 'N' gauge ready-to-run model with factory-fitted digital sound - a two-car Class 108 Diesel Multiple Unit. Finished in BR blue with full yellow ends, the model contained a 6-pin Zimo MX646N sound decoder in the powered vehicle and a 6-pin Zimo MX681N decoder in the trailer. Not only did it sound good, but the driving functionality was excellent too.

On the rolling stock front, Hornby delivered its 'OO' gauge rebuilt LSWR 58ft Maunsell non-corridor stock. Four different vehicle types were issued including six-compartment Lavatory Brake Third, six-compartment Lavatory Brake Composite, nine-compartment Lavatory Third and an eight-compartment Brake Third. Each appeared in Southern Railway olive green and BR crimson.

Whilst not quite so glamorous, Oxford Rail nevertheless plugged a few more important gaps with the addition of two more ready-to-run 'OO' wagon types including the LNER 10ton cattle wagon and LNER six-plank open wagon. Both were well proportioned with plenty of rivet and plank detail, together with turned metal buffers, metal wheels and nicely detailed chassis.

Striking and colourful, Bachmann's 'OO' gauge 23ton BR covered hopper wagon ('Covhop') re-appeared as an exclusive for The Model Centre with Sugar branding, decorated in BR ice blue. It featured revised details accurately reflecting the vehicles used for sugar traffic.

August

DJ Models' (DJM) 'OO' gauge Hunslet 'Austerity' 0-6-0ST arrived in August marking the manufacturer's first home-grown release. Review samples included standard DJM releases and limited edition models, with each appearing refined with plenty of detail differences incorporated such as smokebox doors, chimneys, steps, bunkers and more.

Another popular arrival was the Bachmann- »

63983
RA 6
BRITISH RAILWAYS

Revolution Trains' crowd-funded TEA bogie tanker.

produced 'OO' gauge USA 'S100' 0-6-0T for Bauer Media. Built during the Second World War, these austere American locomotives operated within the Southampton Docks complex for many years, as well as in industrial service. Surefooted on test, our sample hauled seven Mk 1 carriages on the level and ran incredibly quietly and smoothly too.

For larger scale modellers, Heljan delivered its 'O' gauge BR Sulzer Class 25 model of these go-anywhere diesel locomotives. Our review samples in BR blue from Heljan and plain BR green

from Tower Models featured twin motors with flywheels, all-wheel drive, detailed bogies, rotating roof fans and illuminated headcodes.

September

Two new 'N' gauge locomotives and a brand new 'N' gauge wagon were amongst the new arrivals in the *Hornby Magazine* office during September.

Dapol's 'N' gauge Class 33 Bo-Bo diesel-electric impressed with its well-proportioned body capturing the look of the BR Southern Region

prototypes well. Performance appeared excellent, handling an eight-coach rake of BR Mk 1s on *Hornby Magazine's* office test layout with ease.

The manufacturer's much-requested valance-fitted Gresley 'A4' class 'Pacific' was equally well-received, the model appearing just so from all viewing angles. Build quality was excellent as was the overall decoration, our example of 4490 *Empire of India* being finished in LNER garter blue with silver numbers.

September also heralded the arrival of Revolution Trains' first fully crowd-funded model, a modern-era 'N' gauge TEA bogie tank wagon. Available in a choice of colourful contemporary

Brush prototype D0280 *Falcon* **looked superb in 'O' gauge, as produced by Heljan.**

Oxford Rail LNER 10ton cattle wagon.

Bachmann provided a new DCC-ready chassis for its LMS Ivatt '2MT' 2-6-2T in 'OO'.

Above: **Heljan's 'O' gauge Class 24 in plain green as a limited edition for Tower Models.**

Below: **Bachmann's Graham Farish 'N' gauge GWR '64XX' 0-6-0PT.**

liveries it featured etched metal catwalks, finely moulded underframe and turned metal wheels. Produced to order for the company by Rapido Trains, a limited quantity was also made available through selected retailers.

Offering something a little different, OO Works released its latest hand-built 'OO' gauge ready-to-run model in the form of the Great Northern Railway (Ireland) (GNR(I)) 'U' 4-4-0 205 *Down* in GNR(I) lined blue and scarlet.

Hornby took delivery of its TTS-fitted HST power car pack just in time to celebrate the prototype's 40th anniversary in front-line passenger service. Decorated in Virgin Trains East Coast (VTEC) livery, the on-board TTS audio files replicated the MTU sounds well in each power car with 25 functions available to DCC users. A non-sound fitted VTEC liveried model carrying *National Railway Museum 40 Years 1975-2015* nameplates and branding was also produced exclusively for Locomotion Models.

Finally, for modellers of the contemporary scene Locomotion Models released its specially commissioned Hornby 'OO' gauge *Flying Scotsman* train pack, containing 60103 in its present day BR lined green guise with a high gloss finish, together with a BR Mk 1 support coach carrying National Railway Museum lettering.

The year ahead

2016 was another busy and exciting year of model developments and releases with plenty still to come. Before the year end, Bachmann's 'OO' gauge Wickham trolley will have arrived with stockists while Hornby's 'OO' gauge LNER Holden 'B12' 4-6-0 and Peckett 'W4' 0-4-0ST were also expected in the final few weeks of 2016. Also imminent is Dapol's 'O' gauge Class 08 diesel shunter and 10ft wheelbase wagons, 'OO' gauge Black Label Gresley 'A4' 4-6-2 with DCC sound and smoke and, for contemporary modellers, its 'OO' gauge model of Direct Rail Services' Class 68 in a choice of colourful liveries.

Oxford Rail is soon to release its 'OO' gauge GWR 'Dean Goods' 0-6-0 while DCC sound-fitted examples of its 'OO' LSWR Adams '0415' 4-4-2T were also due too. DJ Models' crowd-funded 'OO' gauge Class 71 Bo-Bo electric was also expected to dock before the year end.

But it's not just the traditional manufacturers with projects coming to fruition as Kernow Model Rail Centre's BR Southern Region Class 438 4-TC unit, manufactured on its behalf by Bachmann, was expected early 2017 while Hatton's of Liverpool's 'OO' GWR '14XX' 0-4-2T will form its next locomotive release and the Little Loco Company's 'O' gauge Class 15 was also imminent. Despite so many popular subjects already being available in ready-to-run form, the roster of forthcoming releases shows there are certainly exciting times ahead! ∎

● **For a full listing of forthcoming locomotive projects see pages 120-127.**

Passenger tank
DEVELOPMENT

In the later days of steam operation local passenger services were almost universally hauled by powerful tank locomotives, and they were essential for the successful running of the railways, as **EVAN GREEN-HUGHES** describes.

Gresley 'N2' 0-6-2T 69575 bursts out of Copenhagen tunnel with empty stock from King's Cross in 1952. These powerful tank engines were tasked with empty stock and tightly timed stopping trains on the Great Northern Main Line.
Frank Hebron/Rail Archive Stephenson.

FOR ANY STEAM ENGINE TO operate successfully a method has to be found for it to carry sufficient coal and water to complete its journey. Early railway engines achieved this by mounting a barrel carrying water on a separate vehicle which also had space for coal and this was called a tender. The drawback with this arrangement was that when the engine reached the end of its journey the engine had to be turned to face the other way, or the return journey had to be made with the tender propelled in front of the locomotive, a practice that caused frequent derailments on the uncertain permanent way of the period.

Only a few years after the first faltering engines took to the tracks the Great Western Railway's (GWR) Daniel Gooch was faced with providing motive power for the broad gauge South Devon Railway, a line that abounded in steep gradients and sharp curves. To accomplish this he wished to provide a compact engine that was powerful yet which had most of its weight available for adhesion.

As a result, in 1849 Swindon Works turned out the first of a number of 4-4-0STs designed to take over the principal passenger workings on the route. These featured an unusual arrangement of swivelling front bogie and were provided with one set of flangeless driving wheels to assist them in negotiating sharp corners. So successful was this design that variations of it remained in traffic right until the end of the broad gauge in 1892.

The Bristol and Exeter Railway also adopted the tank layout in 1853 for its passenger trains, although this time of the 4-2-4T type. These locomotives featured a giant driving wheel of 9ft diameter with a four wheel bogie at each end and were intended primarily for express work. While they were only moderately successful they did prove the suitability for passenger services of an engine that had a bogie at each end.

As might be expected, as locomotives became larger and the distances between stops greater, more fuel and water had to be carried and for this reason the use of tank engines for long-distance express services declined. However, by the mid 19th century the cities of the UK were growing at an incredible pace and with this growth came a demand for urban travel, a demand that was satisfied by providing high frequency trains into and out of major stations, work that was ideally suited for haulage by tank engines. At this stage there was not universal agreement as to which wheel arrangement would be best suited for this work and even within the GWR there were two different schools of thought.

Wolverhampton Works came up with the '517', which was an 0-4-2T with an open cab, the first of which appeared in 1868 while Swindon preferred the 2-4-0T, the first of which came **»**

"In 1849 Swindon Works turned out the first of a number of 4-4-0ST designs."

EVAN GREEN-HUGHES

NER Fletcher 'G6' 0-4-4T shunts a sleeping car outside York station in 1924. These venerable looking locomotives had a well tank between the frames for water. P.F. Cooke/Rail Archive Stephenson.

into service the following year as the '455' class. Both types proved to be sufficiently powerful for suburban and secondary passenger duties and remained in production for around 30 years.

Other railways faced with the same requirement came up with other solutions. The St Helen's Railway went for a 2-4-2T in 1863, as did the London & North Western (LNWR) and the Great Eastern while the 4-4-0T was preferred by the North London and Metropolitan railways. However it was to be the 0-4-4T that was to find the greatest favour in the mid-19th century and so popular was this wheel configuration that Kitson of Leeds offered a standard passenger version straight from its catalogue by 1877.

The 0-4-4T design had the advantage that side tanks could be used but these could be set sufficiently far back so that it was still possible to gain access to the inside motion while still providing a low centre of gravity. Amongst the users of this style of passenger tank were the Lancashire & Yorkshire (LYR), South Eastern & Chatham, Great Northern and Midland railways.

Each of these designs had its own advantages and disadvantages. Locomotives fitted with outside cylinders tended to give a rough ride to passengers when worked hard, while those with cylinders inside the frames were more difficult to maintain. Those fitted with saddle tanks had a higher centre of gravity and rolled more than those fitted with side tanks, but the former made it easier to access the motion of inside cylinders.

Back on the GWR, the great railway company eventually opted for 'pannier' tanks mounted on the boiler sides for most of its tank engines – an arrangement that kept the centre of gravity low, made maintenance relatively easy, and still allowed a good amount of water to be carried. Engines that were required to run bunker first a great deal benefitted from a set of trailing wheels, although these reduced the weight available for adhesion, while a set of bogie wheels at the front proved a distinct advantage when running at more than a modest speed. It seemed as though no one design was ideal for all duties and that as yet the perfect passenger tank locomotive had yet to be designed.

A major development

The next significant development came from the London, Tilbury & Southend Railway (LTS) in 1880 which introduced a 4-4-2T outside cylinder design with side tanks and was specifically manufactured to cope with the unique requirements of the railway. The LTS had a main line of only 39 miles but it had frequent station stops and these served communities housing some of the wealthiest of London's commuters. Trains were heavy, often of 400tons, but ran to express timings, services were frequent and space at the termini was at a premium.

The first batches of these engines were constructed by Sharp Stewart and Co and Nasmyth, Wilson and Co with 36 being introduced over 12 years. These were subsequently followed by others in which the driving wheels were progressively increased in size from 6ft 1in to 6ft 6in, the cylinders increased in width by 1in and from the 1909 batch also having larger boilers.

Two years later this wheel arrangement was adopted by William Adams of the London & South Western Railway (LSWR) who was looking for something more satisfactory than the company's 4-4-0s for suburban work. His '415' class, better known as the Adams 'Radial', eventually ran to 71 engines and proved most satisfactory, although like many outside cylinder designs could give a rough ride to passengers when under acceleration.

The London & North Western Railway (LNWR) took up the idea with FW Webb converting 10 ex-Metropolitan 4-4-0Ts to this wheel arrangement in 1892. He followed this up some years later with the 4-4-2T 'Precursor' tanks which proved such a success on suburban routes out of Euston that they virtually monopolised this work until the early 1930s. A similar development next door at King's Cross had seen the Great Northern Railway (GNR) adopting the 4-4-2T with the first appearing in 1898 from designer HA Ivatt and with the type eventually being used on the majority of the London commuter services as well as elsewhere.

Even the newly-formed Great Central Railway

(GCR) got in on the act and the first locomotives built by the company at their Gorton works were also 4-4-2Ts for passenger work. The 'C12s' began to appear in 1903 and were used not only on commuter services out of Marylebone but also all over the GCR system as well as on the routes administered by the Cheshire Lines Committee. These engines had smaller driving wheels than the LTS 4-4-2Ts, which gave them considerable tractive effort and great acceleration.

4-4-2Ts remained popular throughout the Victorian era, particularly with the London Brighton & South Coast Railway (LBSCR), which began constructing the type in 1906 to the design of Earle Marsh. Four different types, classes '11'-'14', had emerged by 1909, all provided with inside cylinders but these proved troublesome at first being poor performers and did not prove entirely satisfactory until provided with bigger boilers in Southern Railway days.

The GWR built a 4-4-2T version of its 4-4-0 »

BR '4MT' 2-6-4T 80122 leaves Stirling with the 3.39pm to Edinburgh Princes Street in September 1960. These fine locomotives owed their heritage to the Fowler and Stanier 2-6-4T designs of the 1930s. W.J. Verden Anderson/Rail Archive Stephenson.

'County' in 1903 for suburban work around London and Birmingham. The '2221' class was successful enough but unlike those built for the LBSCR was not to enjoy a long life as the GWR preferred six-coupled and 2-6-2T locomotives and so the class was all withdrawn by 1925. Like many other classes of outside-cylinder 4-4-2 these machines suffered from rough riding.

The problems of poor riding were such that many designers were not satisfied that the outside cylinder 4-4-2Ts offered the best solution to secondary passenger work. Even though by f1888 William Adams' LSWR suburban engines were only six years old, issues with ride quality were such that he introduced an alternative with his 'T1' 0-4-4T, which had inside cylinders and much smoother running too.

Locomotives of this wheel arrangement were introduced to the Midland Railway by 1875 under Samuel Johnson and more than 200 had been constructed by this time but most of these were employed on secondary duties rather than those serving heavy commuter flows. By the mid-1880s the LYR also had around 50 of

> *"By this time the 0-6-2T was favoured for heavy suburban work."*
>
> **EVAN GREEN-HUGHES**

the type, although again engaged on lighter suburban duties.

By contrast Adams' engines were designed from the outset for heavy suburban work and these were followed by an even more successful design which appeared in 1897 after Dugald Drummond had succeeded him as Chief Mechanical Engineer. The 'M7' 0-4-4T with its 4ft 8½ in driving wheels, large boiler and considerable tractive effort eventually ran to 105 examples, some of which remained in service until 1965.

One of the successful designs of 0-4-4Ts was Fletcher's 'G6' for the North Eastern Railway (NER). These engines were not built for heavy stop/ start commuter operations but were intended for branch line passenger service. One unusual feature of these engines was the provision of a well tank for water which meant that neither side tanks nor a saddle tank were provided, giving a very low centre of gravity. After a brief flirtation with 2-4-2Ts, the NER went back to the 0-4-4T under Wilson Worsdell with the introduction of the 'G5', a design that ran to 110 examples and which lasted until 1958.

More power

The last few years of the 19th century produced a requirement for more powerful locomotives for suburban duties, and for this many railways elected to use the 0-6-2T. In many respects this was a logical step forward for, by providing an additional driving axle, a larger boiler could be provided and more tractive effort supplied than was possible with the 0-4-4T.

The LYR based a number of its earliest engines of this type on designs by Kitson of Leeds and two versions were produced, those intended for passenger work having larger driving wheels and consequently a better turn of speed. Other railways, such as the Manchester, Sheffield & Lincolnshire (later the Great Central Railway), also introduced some of this type but these were more commonly used on goods or shunting duties.

This remained the case until the early years of the 20th century when HA Ivatt produced a superb suburban passenger tank for the GNR. The 'N1' was intended for hauling heavy suburban trains into and out of London and also for the hilly country of the industrial West Riding of Yorkshire. These inside cylinder engines, which first made an appearance in 1907, had 4ft 8in boilers and 5ft 8in wheels with a wheelbase of 23ft 9in which

A LNWR 'Whale' 4-4-2T powers away from Wembley Central with a Euston-Watford Junction working shortly before the introduction of electric trains in the early 1920s.
Rail Archive Stephenson.

made them very large compared with what had gone before. In fact they were so large that they proved too heavy for the Metropolitan Widened Lines, and subsequent batches had the rear wheels, side tanks and coal bunker remodelled to move the weight towards the rear and lessen the axle load at the front.

After the First World War, Ivatt's successor Nigel Gresley carefully evaluated all the potential contenders for suburban passenger tanks and came down in favour of the 'N1', producing his own version, the 'N2', a design that was later adopted by the London and North Eastern Railway (LNER) as a group standard. These locomotives were used not only around London, but Scotland, Nottingham and the West Riding.

By this time the 0-6-2 tank was favoured for heavy suburban work, with the 0-4-4T for lighter duties and the 4-4-2T for faster trains. However there still wasn't universal agreement. Many designers felt that to get the best out of a passenger tank a leading and a trailing carrying wheel was essential to ensure smooth running and to reduce flange wear. The LYR's Chief Mechanical Engineer John Aspinall came up with an elegant 2-4-2T in 1886 with inside cylinders and side tanks which was to be the first member of his famous '1008' class, a design »

Aspinall '1008' 2-4-2T 50802 waits to leave Fleetwood with a train for Blackpool North on September 6 1948. John P. Wilson/Rail Archive Stephenson.

GWR '517' 0-4-2T 835 and another stand at Swindon shed in 1928. These early GWR tank engines were an important step in the development of passenger tank design. J.N. Maskelyne/Rail Archive Stephenson

The 4-4-2 wheel arrangement found much favour in early 20th century tank engine design, and particularly in the Midlands and East. LNER 'C12' 4-4-2T 1517N (early LNER numbering) poses at Nottingham Victoria in 1923. Gordon Hepburn/Rail Archive Stephenson.

The LTS line 4-4-2Ts were masters of their territory until the advent of a more modern three-cylinder 2-6-4T created by Stanier. Ex-LTS '3P' 41943 saw out its final years in rural Nottinghamshire where it arrives at Bulwell with a Nottingham Midland to Worksop train in 1954.
T.G. Hepburn/Rail Archive Stephenson.

that proved capable of both hard work and fast, smooth running particularly in the hilly Pennine districts. This was a relatively big locomotive which was fitted with a 4ft 1in diameter boiler and driving wheels of 5ft 8in diameter and was eventually to stretch to more than 270 locomotives, many of which survived until almost the end of steam.

Six-coupled tanks

Despite the success of the 2-4-2T, many designers wished to see a locomotive with six coupled wheels employed on passenger work and so it was left to perhaps the greatest of locomotive engineers to come up with the definitive design.

In 1904 George Jackson Churchward of the GWR produced the first of what was to become almost an industry standard, the 2-6-2T. The '44XX' was intended for lighter trains, while the '31XX' which followed two years later was a bigger design for heavier commuter work. Both were well laid out engines with two simple to maintain outside cylinders, taper boiler, side tanks and 5ft 8in driving wheels. So good was this basic concept that production of these and their derivatives was to last until 1950.

Not all attempts to provide larger passenger tanks met with the same level of success. For handling expresses, Richard Maunsell of the Southern Railway built the 'River' 2-6-4Ts in 1925, which were fitted with three cylinders and an extremely large boiler. These proved to be masters of the work for which they had been intended but unfortunately were unstable on poor track, resulting in a bad accident at Sevenoaks in 1927 when *River Cray* derailed at 55mph killing 13 passengers. They were subsequently converted to tender engines.

In 1930 Sir Henry Fowler of the London Midland & Scottish Railway (LMS) built a 2-6-2T which dimensionally had much in common with the GWR design, although it featured a parallel boiler. 70 of these were produced. He also more importantly came up with a 2-6-4T which was designed for longer distance commuter trains and proved to be a very smooth-riding design with

good coal and water capacity and in turn a very useful range.

The use of a four-wheel bogie at the rear resulted in greater stability when running backwards but also enabled the use of longer frames and the provision of a larger coal bunker. A total of 125 were produced in a number of different batches and so successful was the concept that it was adapted and improved to form the basis of some of the last steam engines to be built.

The final generations

Shortly after this William Stanier was headhunted by the LMS from the GWR and he brought with him many of the best ideas from Swindon, including boiler design, which he subsequently superimposed on the best that the company already had. These included the 2-6-2T and the 2-6-4T passenger tanks, improved versions of which were turned out in 1935, being very similar to the earlier engines although provided with taper boilers and improved cab layouts. An interesting improvement was a series of three-cylinder 2-6-4Ts for the LTS route that replaced the 4-4-2Ts which had lasted for more than 50 years on such duties. Despite all these improvements there was still room for a small class of 10 0-4-4Ts with push-pull gear specifically for use on minor branch line passenger services.

As the 1930s drew on the 2-6-2T and 2-6-4Ts became to be seen as the industry standard for new build, although all companies continued to operate locomotives of other wheel configurations. The LNER stuck with its 0-6-2Ts until 1928 when Gresley produced the 'V1' 2-6-2T, a powerful machine used in London but mainly in the North East and Scotland. Although 71 were built of this and the 'V3' variant they did not displace the 0-6-2T which continued in use.

Throughout this period the LMS and to a lesser extent the GWR actively replaced second string tank and tender locomotives with more modern 2-6-2Ts and 2-6-4Ts (in the former case – the GWR never operated any 2-6-4Ts) and the LNER added a further 100 2-6-4Ts of Thompson's 'L1'

> *"In the 1930s 2-6-2T and 2-6-4Ts became industry standards."*
>
> **EVAN GREEN-HUGHES**

design before all investment was halted for the war years.

Nationalisation saw the introduction of a scheme to provide standard designs to be shared by all regions and once these emerged they were found to be heavily based on the former products of the LMS. Amongst these were three tank designs, although all were intended for mixed traffic duties as required.

The Standard '4MT' 2-6-4T tank was an upgraded version of the LMS' Fairburn design, which owed its ancestry to the Fowler engines of 1930, and was used extensively on all types of traffic including semi-express passenger on the LTS as well as on single-coach locals on the Killin branch in Scotland. The '3MT' 2-6-2T was for lines where a 16ton axle load was in force. This used a chassis based on LMS practice married with the boiler components of a Swindon No. 4 standard boiler. These engines found a great deal of work on secondary passenger duties, being often found in rural Wales and on empty stock trains. A little '2MT' 2-6-2T was also built, again descended from an LMS design which

Churchward created the template for modern tank engine design with his '44XX' 2-6-2T which led onto a number of future designs on the GWR. '51XX' 2-6-2T 5132 leaves Exeter St Davids with a local train for Torquay on June 5 1949.
John P. Wilson/Rail Archive Stephenson.

was intended to replace various classes of 'auto fitted' locomotives on push-pull duties. Although these were perfectly adequate engines they had a very short life as much of the work for which they had been designed disappeared as a result of closures and what remained soon went over to diesel railcars.

As a result of the modernisation plan and the Beeching cuts, all work for passenger tanks had ceased by 1968 with the last few at work in the north where they worked some secondary trains as well as portions of main line expresses from destinations such as Bradford. Fortunately many survived long enough to be saved for use on our heritage railways, for which work they are ideally suited. Of these most are of the later BR 'Standard' and LMS designs, although there are examples of some older types, such as LSWR and LTS 4-4-2Ts and some of the LNER 0-6-2Ts, not to mention a host of GWR types.

It is still possible on these lines to appreciate these locomotives doing the job for which they were originally designed and hopefully it will be so for many more years to come. ∎

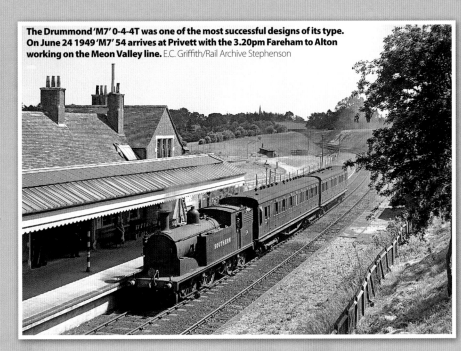

The Drummond 'M7' 0-4-4T was one of the most successful designs of its type. On June 24 1949 'M7' 54 arrives at Privett with the 3.20pm Fareham to Alton working on the Meon Valley line. E.C. Griffith/Rail Archive Stephenson

Grosvenor Square

Layout complete, it's time to learn the ropes for how it will run. **MIKE WILD** discusses how Grosvenor Square will operate, what it will run with and the future plans for this new 'OO' gauge railway.

PHOTOGRAPHY, MIKE WILD

IT'S ONE THING TO BUILD A LAYOUT, but it's another to make it run and get the most from its potential. With its five entry/exit tracks, multiple sidings and sprawling station, there is a huge amount of operational potential in Grosvenor Square which we are all itching to discover and enjoy.

It is a big layout, even in its initial form, with a 12ft scenic section that is set to get bigger in the future with the addition of a planned fourth scenic baseboard. This will include the rest of the approach junction allowing trains from the two inbound tracks to reach any platform as well as the reverse being possible for departing trains.

In its short formation there are limitations in the trackplan which will bring challenges to the operating team – not least in that the rear third of the layout, when viewed from the front, will be almost entirely independent of the rest of the station. Links are planned in the off-scene storage yard, but there are some movements which will then have to take place out of public view.

Each time we have looked at the layout during its construction, conversations have considered how much there is to do on this layout. Up to five operators can easily be swallowed by Grosvenor Square, including one for the storage yard preparing and dispatching trains, two drivers, a panel operator and a

shunter working the rear lines and stabling tracks. It all adds up to an exciting prospect and we can't wait to bring the full layout together for its debut at the Warley National Model Railway Exhibition in November 2016.

One of the elements which makes this layout stand out is actually a traffic type that is missing – goods. Being a city station, goods traffic would have been kept further out, keeping the route free for passenger transport. Parcels traffic would still work into the station, so it will be possible to see four-wheel box vans as part of those formations, but the closest you will see to an actual goods train at Grosvenor Square will be an occasional ballast working. »

1 The station throat offers the potential for multiple train movements. A 'Warship' enters with a rake of Mk 1s as a 'King' departs with Hornby Collett Bow-end stock in parallel with a 'Grange' at the head of a parcels working.

Station movements

There are a number of important movements which we want to replicate on the 'Square during an exhibition running session. Top of the list are arriving and departing trains from the Western Region, followed by parcels workings, multiple units, local stopping trains, empty stock movements, light engines and inter-regional workings.

The main part of the station's business will be arriving and departing express trains. Trains will be limited to six carriages plus a parcels van to fit within the platforms – a train length that we have found to be ample on most of our previous layouts. An arriving train will

draw into Platform 3 or 4 and stop inside the trainshed. The driver will then have to set back a few millimetres to uncouple using the Kadee permanent magnets buried under the track – something we are all going to need practice at. The train engine can then draw forward to clear the stock.

In some cases the station pilot will couple up to the rear of the stock to remove it to the carriage sidings, part of the storage yard design, but in others a fresh engine will be brought into the station to take the same stock straight out as a new departure. In each case once the stock has left the station the original train engine will then be released and

be allowed to move up the platform before departing for the stabling point or locomotive shed – the latter being off scene in the storage yard.

Platforms 5 and 6 will mainly be used as departure platforms where stock released by the pilot engine will be returned for a later formation. Parcels workings will enter and head for Platform 7 prior to shunting and reforming while the two lines beyond Platform 7 will be used for stock storage in the station vicinity.

Local stopping trains will mainly use Platforms 1 and 2 at the leading edge of the layout. These trains will consist of both locomotive hauled and Diesel Multiple Unit ➤➤

PLATFORM

3

2 The 'spotters' have got a rare treat today of a Collett '2884' 2-8-0 working into the station on a ballast working. It will run-round in the loop at the back of the station using Platform 7.

3 'Western' D1000 *Western Enterprise* ticks over under the canopy waiting for a clear road to reverse up the station.

(DMU) formations. DMU stabling sidings are also provided off the end of Platform 1 allowing further movements to take place between these two areas. Run-round facilities are provided between Platforms 1 and 2 with a pair of points allowing locomotives arriving in Platform 2 to uncouple from their stock using the magnets before moving forward into the headshunt. With Platform 1 free, the train engine can then run around its stock and either couple onto the other end ready for departure or depart for servicing off scene.

Light engine movements around the station will be significant as the station pilot will regularly be running around between stock movements on its own while incoming train engines and fresh train engines will be stabled in different platforms to make them available for quick departures. We are also looking forward to recreating the spectacle of an arriving train engine following its stock back up the platform as it departs before being held at the signal for a clear route out - a benefit of using digital control.

Inter-regional

A fun part of the 'Square is that its West Midlands location means we can bring in trains from beyond the Western Region to replicate changes of traction at a regional boundary. This time around, Midland Region traffic will work in from the north to change engines while some trains from the Western Region will be making the return journey.

Taking a Midland train as an example, the train will arrive in Platform 2 or 3 behind suitable motive power – most likely an ex-London Midland & Scottish Railway (LMS) 4-6-0 or a Type 4 diesel – while waiting close by will be a new train engine from the Western Region to take over. Once the Midland Region train has come to a stand and the engine has been uncoupled, the new train engine will back down onto the stock for departure.

Once clear, the Midland Region engine will leave the scenic area of the storage yard for turning and later it will return to the station to work another inter-regional service heading north from Western Region metals.

This type of operation brings the prospect of seeing Western Region locomotives at the head of Midland Region stock, further varying the abilities of the layout to model real railway practice. **»**

⊡4 The Blue Pullman departs for the Midland Region having worked in as a special. On the left a 'Castle' is waiting to depart alongside one of today's station pilots – a '57XX' 0-6-0PT.

📷 5 A Class 105 rumbles into Platform 2 as a Class 42 waits to reverse onto its train.

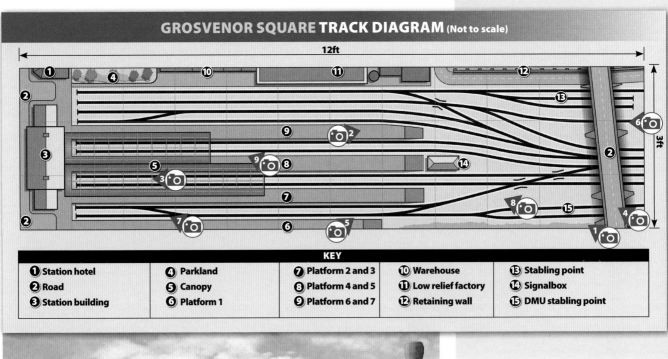

GROSVENOR SQUARE **TRACK DIAGRAM** (Not to scale)

12ft

3ft

	KEY			
❶ Station hotel	**❹** Parkland	**❼** Platform 2 and 3	**❿** Warehouse	**⓭** Stabling point
❷ Road	**❺** Canopy	**❽** Platform 4 and 5	**⓫** Low relief factory	**⓮** Signalbox
❸ Station building	**❻** Platform 1	**❾** Platform 6 and 7	**⓬** Retaining wall	**⓯** DMU stabling point

📷**6** A Collett 'Hall' 4-6-0 makes a steady departure with its rake of parcels vans heading south for London.

📷**7** Collett '4575' 2-6-2T 5550 runs round its stock in the local platforms.

Motive power

Happily the ready-to-run market is highly supportive of the Western Region and there is an impressive range of locomotives already available off the shelf with even more to come in 2017 and beyond.

That range carries everything from a '14XX' 0-4-2T right through to the imposing 'King' 4-6-0. In between there are options to run 'Pannier' and 'Prairie' tanks, 'Dukedog' 4-4-0s and an impressive selection of GWR 4-6-0s including 'Grange', 'Hall', 'Modified Hall', 'Star' and 'Castle'.

The timeframe and location for the 'Square won't allow for everything ever made to be run (although I'm sure we will push the boundaries at times), as we are planning to model the 1960-1965 period in the main. This will cover the final years of steam on the Western Region and the introduction of diesel-hydraulics up to and including the 'Westerns'.

Chief amongst the steam fleet will be 'King', 'Castle' and 'Hall' 4-6-0s for passenger work while a 'Grange' will mainly be in service for parcels traffic. 'Small Prairie' 2-6-2Ts will be used for local

stopping trains while a '57XX' will be allocated as station pilot. A '61XX' 2-6-2T will also be available for station pilot duties should it be required on heavier duties.

The 2015 introduced '64XX' 0-6-0PT from Bachmann will also see service on autotrains while BR Standard 2-6-2T and 2-6-4Ts will be employed on stopping trains too.

Working side by side with the wide-ranging steam fleet will be a raft of diesel-hydraulics including a pair of 'Westerns', three 'Warships', a 'Hymek' and a Class 22. These will also be joined by Brush prototype D0280 *Falcon* (which moved to the Western Region right at the end of our timeframe in 1965) in BR two-tone green to add further variety to the fleet and occasional appearances of a Blue Pullman Diesel Electric Multiple Unit (DEMU). We might even bring BRCW prototype D0260 *Lion* out for an adventure from time to time.

DMUs will consist of Class 101, 105 and 108 two-car sets together with a Class 128 single parcels railcar.

Traffic from the Midland Region will be handled

by 'Royal Scot' and 'Jubilee' 4-6-0s or Class 46 or 47 diesels depending upon requirements. Incoming parcels traffic from the Midland will be in the hands of Stanier 'Black Five' 4-6-0s, a Class 31 or 37 – the latter giving the spotters on the end of Platform 4 something to look out for.

Rolling stock

Passenger coaches will form the vast majority of the stock for the 'Square with passenger sets including Hornby's 2016 released Collett bow-end stock, the same manufacturer's impressive Hawksworth corridor stock and even an ex-GWR 'B-set' in BR livery.

British Railways Mk 1s will also be a popular choice for formations while viewers will also be able to see later Collett corridor stock, autocoaches and BR 57ft suburban carriages on local trains.

Trains coming from the Midland Region will be formed either of BR Mk1 carriages or ex-LMS Stanier 57ft corridor stock, while we also have thoughts about including a 'sleeper' train working from Bristol to Scotland in the stock boxes. »

With plenty of platforms to fill we are sure to need plenty of carriages for Grosvenor Square which will keep the storage yard and scenic section operators equally busy.

Future prospects

What we have here is a complete layout, but not what you would call a finished layout. There is still more which can be done scenically to Grosvenor Square to make it even more detailed and attractive. For example, the low brick wall at the back of the station area really needs capping stones adding to it while the factory buildings will benefit from further weathering too. Then there is the fourth scenic board to be built and more.

Right now as I type at the end of October, our thoughts are turning to development of the storage yard for Grosvenor Square and that will become the focus of a future feature in *Hornby Magazine* following the layout's debut at the Warley National Model Railway Exhibition. The yard we have in mind will be quite different to previous designs we have used as it will allow trains to depart and turn around a full loop before returning to the station later in the sequence through the use of a 'dumbbell' design.

That will take some building, but it will certainly enhance the operating procedure and allow all of the team behind the layout to get stuck into doing what we enjoy the most – running trains both for our entertainment and exhibition visitors alike. ■

THE ROSTER			
Class	**Traffic type**	**Region**	**Manufacturer**
GWR 'King' 4-6-0	Express	Western	Hornby
GWR 'Castle' 4-6-0	Express	Western	Hornby
GWR 'Hall' 4-6-0	Long distance stopping	Western	Bachmann
GWR 'Grange' 4-6-0	Parcels	Western	Hornby
GWR '45XX'/'4575' 2-6-2T	Local stopping	Western	Bachmann
GWR '64XX' 0-6-0PT	Autotrains	Western	Bachmann
GWR '57XX' 0-6-0PT	Station pilot	Western	Bachmann
GWR '2251' 0-6-0	Vans and ballast	Western	Bachmann
GWR '61XX' 2-6-2T	Local stopping/station pilot	Western	Hornby
LMS 'Royal Scot' 4-6-0	Express	Midland	Hornby
LMS 'Jubilee' 4-6-0	Express	Midland	Bachmann
BR 'Britannia' 4-6-2	Express	Western/Midland	Hornby
BR '3MT' 2-6-2T	Local stopping	Western	Bachmann
BR '4MT' 2-6-4T	Local stopping	Western/Midland	Bachmann
Class 08	Shunting	Western	Hornby
Class 22	Parcels/vans	Western	Dapol
Class 35 'Hymek'	Stopping/parcels	Western	Heljan
Class 31	Parcels	Midland	Hornby
Class 37	Parcels	Midland	Bachmann
Class 42 'Warship'	Express	Western	Bachmann
Class 43 'Warship'	Express	Western	Bachmann
Class 46	Express	Midland	Bachmann
Class 47	Express	Midland	Bachmann
Class 52 'Western'	Express	Western	Heljan/Dapol
Class 53 *Falcon*	Express	Western	Heljan
Class 101	Local stopping	Midland	Bachmann
Class 108	Local stopping	Western	Bachmann
Class 128	Parcels	Western	Bachmann
Blue Pullman	Express/special working	Midland	Bachmann

⦿8 **GWR 'King'** **6029** *King Edward VIII* **departs Grosvenor Square for London. The lower quadrant semaphore signals are Dapol models operated by Train-Tech decoders.**

Above: **A 'Hymek' has charge of a short local working formed of Collett stock alongside a Class 108 under the shortened canopy.**

Forward

A staggering 88 new locomotive models are in development right now. **MIKE WILD** looks ahead

IT NEVER CEASES TO AMAZE JUST how many models have been selected for development. Right now there are almost 90 new locomotive projects ranging in progress from proposal through engineering samples and final production models moving around the world to reach the shops.

By comparison with 2015, 2016 has been a slower year. Announcements have come through readily, but not in the same abundant quantities, while delivery of new products has also been steady throughout the year.

Leading the way in delivery of new products

during 2016 is Hornby. The manufacturer has clearly resolved its production issues in China with delivery of the final locomotives from its 2015 range and, more importantly, all but one of the 2016 plan expected to arrive before Christmas.

Bachmann has seen a year of consolidation in 'OO' and 'N' scales with only one new ready-to-run locomotive delivered for 'OO' by late October as we brought this survey together. In 'N' gauge it has released a pair of new tank engines in the GWR '64XX' 0-6-0PT and BR '4MT' 2-6-4T and is now close to delivering its GWR 'Castle' 4-6-0. The company is working hard to reduce the backlog

of projects and hopefully in the New Year we will see a steady stream of Bachmann branded new products arriving in the shops.

Dapol is also moving ahead with delivery of two new 'N' gauge locomotives during the year alongside its second 'O' gauge engine in the Class 08 and, perhaps most significantly, its Warley 2015 announced Black Label 'A4' 4-6-2 which is due to arrive for sale in November.

Elsewhere, Heljan has been ploughing its own furrow in 'O' gauge with a stream of new projects being revealed while new names in the sector are delivering too. Oxford Rail launched its Adams 'Radial' 4-4-2T in November 2015 and

Kernow Model Rail Centre's unpowered Southern Region 4-TC is expected to be available in the first quarter of 2017.

to 2017 »»

to 2017 and evaluates what our manufacturers have to offer in the future.

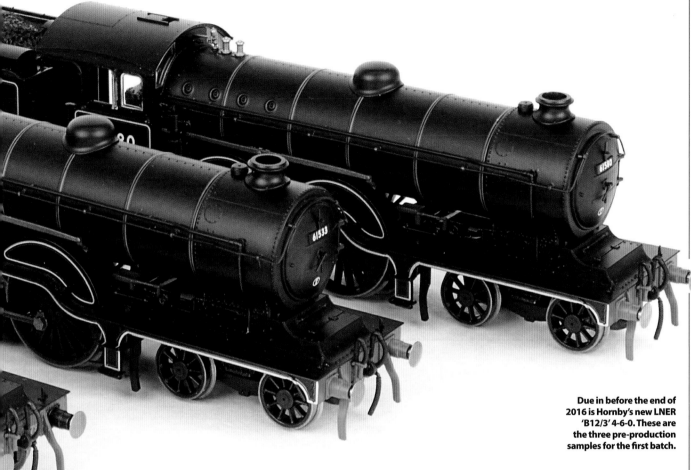

Due in before the end of 2016 is Hornby's new LNER 'B12/3' 4-6-0. These are the three pre-production samples for the first batch.

followed it with new wagons during the summer while Rapido Trains, through Locomotion Models, released its first British outline product in the APT-E. Also new to the scene, although only in name, is Sutton's Locomotive Works (SLW), which wowed modellers with its announcement and delivery of its outstanding model of the BR Class 24 on the same day.

Even considering all this, there is much to look forward to in 2017, as we will show.

'OO' gauge

The past 12 months has seen 12 new locomotives arrive for 'OO' gauge ranging from the compact Hornby 'J50' 0-6-0T to the superbly detailed SLW Class 24 and Hornby's Raven 'Q6' 0-8-0.

The Great Western Railway's locomotive designs are still clearly in favour for 'OO' with almost 50% of the in-development steam products modelling its motive power. The list includes '1361' 0-6-0STs and a steam railmotor from Kernow Model Rail Centre, the fabulous '47XX' 2-8-0 from Heljan, »

TABLE 1 - 'OO' GAUGE NEW RELEASES FOR – 2016-2017			
Class	**Region**	**Manufacturer**	**Expected**
GWR steam railmotor	Western	Kernow MRC	TBA
GWR 'Dean Goods' 0-6-0	Western	Oxford Rail	2016
GWR '1361' 0-6-0ST	Western	Kernow MRC	TBA
GWR '1361' 0-6-0ST	Western	Heljan	2017
GWR '1366' 0-6-0PT	Western	Heljan	2017
GWR '14XX' 0-4-2T	Western	Hatton's	2016
GWR '47XX' 2-8-0	Western	Heljan	2017
GWR 'King' 4-6-0	Western	Hatton's	2017
GWR '94XX' 0-6-0PT	Western	Bachmann	2017
LSWR 'B4' 0-4-0T	Southern	Dapol	TBA
LBSCR 'H2' 4-4-2T	Southern	Bachmann	2017
SECR 'H' 0-4-4T	Southern	Hornby	2017
SR 'Merchant Navy' 4-6-2	Southern	Hornby	2017
LNWR 'Coal Tank' 0-6-2T	Midland	Bachmann	2017
LMS '5MT' 2-6-0	Midland	Bachmann	2017
GNR Stirling single 4-2-2	Eastern	Rapido Trains/ Locomotion	TBA
LNER 'A4' 4-6-2	Eastern	Dapol (Black Label)	2016
LNER 'B12' 4-6-0	Eastern	Hornby	2016
LNER 'V2' 2-6-2	Eastern	Bachmann	TBA
Hudswell Clarke 0-6-0ST	Industrial	DJ Models	TBA
Peckett 'W4' 0-4-0ST	Industrial	Hornby	2016
AEC GWR railcar	Western	Dapol	2017
Bulleid 10201-10203	Southern	Kernow MRC	TBA
Class 07	Southern	Heljan	TBA
Class 21/29	Scottish	Dapol	TBA
Class 24/1	Various	Bachmann	TBA
Class 41 'Warship'	Western	Kernow MRC	TBA
Class 41 prototype HST	Western	Locomotion/ Rapido Trains	TBA
Class 59	Western	Dapol	2017
Class 68	Various	Dapol	2016
Class 71	Southern	DJ Models	2016
Class 74	Southern	DJ Models	2016
Class 70/8	Various	Bachmann	2017
Class 90	Various	Bachmann	TBA
Class 92	Various	DJ Models	TBA
Class 117	Various	Bachmann	TBA
Class 121	Various	Bachmann	TBA
Class 121	Various	Dapol	TBA
Class 122	Various	Dapol	TBA
Class 158	Various	Bachmann	TBA
Class 414 2-HAP	Southern	Bachmann	TBA
Class 438 4-TC	Southern	Kernow/Bachmann	2017
Class 450	Southern	Bachmann	2017
Janus 0-6-0 diesel shunter	Industrial	Golden Valley Hobbies	2017
L&B 2-6-2T ('009')	Southern	Heljan	2016
Baldwin 4-6-0T ('009')	Industrial	Bachmann	TBA

Hatton's 'King' and '14XX', and Bachmann's proposed Hawksworth '94XX' 0-6-0PT.

However, the next model set to arrive of Western origin is Oxford Rail's 'Dean Goods' 0-6-0. The new manufacturer is making great strides both in developing its products and meeting expectations for delivery timescales and quality. As we closed for press the 0-6-0 was already on its way to the UK with arrival expected either in the final weeks of 2016 or the first month of 2017.

The Southern Railway has a strong showing too with the latest announcement being the South Eastern and Chatham Railway 'H' 0-4-4T by Hornby. This is scheduled for release in the second half of 2017 following on from the air-smoothed 'Merchant Navy' which is due to arrive in the first quarter of the year.

Bachmann still has its model of the 'Brighton Atlantic' in development with an engineering sample expected to arrive at its Leicestershire headquarters as this book went to press. Bachmann is also catering for London Midland & Scottish Railway (LMS) modellers with its London

& North Western Railway 'Coal Tank' and Stanier 'Mogul' both making progress. The 'Mogul' will be first with projections of February 2017 for arrival while the 'Coal Tank' is to follow later in the year.

Hornby is set to satisfy both Great Eastern Railway and industrial modellers before the end of 2016 with its models of the Peckett 'W4' 0-4-0ST and LNER 'B12/3' 4-6-0 expected to arrive in November and December bringing to a close its 2016 catalogue - except for the 'Merchant Navy', which has been deferred to 2017.

On the diesel front, a handful of new announcements have been made ranging from the Class 07 diesel shunter by Heljan to the prototype High Speed Train power cars by Locomotion Models, a Class 414 2-HAP by Bachmann and a crowd-funded Class 92 through DJ Models. Although not strictly fitting in with this survey as it is unpowered, Kernow Model Rail Centre is also expecting to release its model of the Southern Region 4-TC trailer unit in the first months of 2017.

Making good progress is Dapol's Class 59,

Dapol was expecting decorated samples of its 'OO' scale GWR AEC railcar in the autumn.

Heljan's 'OO' gauge GWR '1366' 0-6-0PT appeared as a first sample at the Warley exhibition in November 2015. Release is expected in 2017.

which broke cover as an engineering sample during August while its Class 68 is also approaching completion with final livery details being corrected during September and October before production. DJ Models is also expected to release its crowd-funded Class 71 model before the end of the year while it is also working on a follow up in the Class 74 electro-diesels – themselves rebuilds by BR from the Class 71.

Across the board there are now 46 new locomotives proposed or in development for 'OO' gauge consisting of 21 steam and 25 diesel. That's a lot to look forward to and you can find the full list in Table 1.

'N' gauge

The smaller of the three scales in this survey had something of a quiet year in 2016 for locomotive delivery and announcement, but it did witness an important moment when Revolution Trains became the first manufacturer to release a crowd-funded British outline model with the arrival of its

'N' gauge TEA 100ton tanker during early October. It has proved the concept of crowd-funding and is paving the way for more projects produced with the same backing. Revolution revealed its plans to produce the Class 92 Co-Co electric in early October to follow the Class 321 and 390 Electric Multiple Units.

Crowd-funding is becoming a popular option for niche models and DJ Models has added one new project to its 'N' gauge tally with its announcement of a similar scheme to support production of a '92' for the scale.

While DJ Models has released its first 'OO' gauge locomotive in the Hunslet 'Austerity' 0-6-0T, it still has a number of projects on the drawing boards for 'N' including the GWR '43XX' 2-6-0, LNER 'Q6' 0-8-0, Hudswell Clarke 0-6-0ST and Class 17 and 23 diesels.

Bachmann's Graham Farish brand only saw one new announcement in 2016 in the Class 319 Electric Multiple Unit (EMU), but it joins the queue behind the soon to be released GWR

'Castle' 4-6-0 and Class 40 diesel. Both of the latter two will employ new technology as they are to be the first ready-to-run UK outline 'N' gauge models to be equipped with a Next18 DCC decoder socket. In combination with this both are also being designed with digital sound in mind with a factory sound version of the 'Castle' using a Zimo decoder planned to follow its first 'N' gauge sound model – the Class 108 of September.

Dapol meanwhile is working through its list of projects by delivering the SR 'Schools' 4-4-0, Class 33 and valance fitted 'A4' 4-6-2, with one very significant production plan being announced during the year – the prototype HST as a bookset containing power and trailer cars. Still in progress are the Bulleid 'Light Pacifics' in air-smoothed and rebuilt condition, the 'J72' 0-6-0T and diesel classes 50, 59, 68 and 142.

In late October the tally of 'N' gauge projects stood at 23 consisting of nine steam locomotive and 14 diesel and electrics. See Table 2 for the full listing. ››

Dapol is pushing forward with its 'OO' gauge Class 59.

Shunters are a popular subject for 'O' with Heljan developing both the Class 03 and 05. This is the first sample of the Class 05.

'O' gauge

The lure of 'O' gauge appears to have bitten British modellers and manufacturers hard in 2016 with a 100% increase in the number of new projects on the table. The year started with a healthy 10 locomotive models proposed and in development, but in late October that had risen to an impressive 20 covering a mixture of steam and diesel prototypes.

Five new locomotives have been released for the scale during 2016 ranging in size from the diminutive debut model from Minerva Model Railways – the Peckett 'E' 0-4-0ST - through to giants of the main line like the 'Warship' diesel-hydraulic and Brush prototype *Falcon*.

Heljan has been particularly prolific with its announcements following arrival of new names on the scene, staking its claim to production of one new locomotive per quarter during 2017 and forging plans to develop a range of Diesel Multiple Units covering classes 117, 120, 121 and 128 progressively in the future.

However, even though it has a strong and well known reputation for diesel models in 'O' gauge, Heljan is also tackling new ground with its first steam locomotives for the scale. It plans to produce the '61XX' 2-6-2T and '43XX' 2-6-0 »

Newly announced by Hornby in late September is the SECR 'H' 0-4-4T for 2017.

TABLE 2 · 'N' GAUGE NEW RELEASES FOR 2016-2017			
Class	**Region**	**Manufacturer**	**Expected**
GWR 'Castle' 4-6-0	Western	Bachmann	2017
GWR '43XX' 2-6-0	Western	DJ Models	2016
SR 'West Country' 4-6-2	Southern	Dapol	TBA
SR rebuilt 'West Country' 4-6-2	Southern	Dapol	TBA
LNER 'J72' 0-6-0T	Eastern	Dapol	TBA
LNER 'J72' 0-6-0T	Eastern	Bachmann	TBA
LNER 'Q6' 0-8-0	Eastern	DJ Models	TBA
Hunslet 'J94' 0-6-0ST	Eastern	DJ Models	TBA
Hudswell Clarke 0-6-0ST	Industrial	DJ Models	TBA
Class 17	Eastern/Scottish	DJ Models	TBA
Class 23	Eastern	DJ Models	TBA
Class 40	Midland/Eastern	Bachmann	2017
Class 41 prototype HST	Western/Midland	Dapol	2017
Class 50	Midland/Western	Dapol	TBA
Class 59	Western	DJ Models	TBA
Class 59	Western	Dapol	TBA
Class 68	Various	Dapol	TBA
Class 92	Various	DJ Models	TBA
Class 92	Various	Revolution Trains	TBA
Class 142	Midland/Eastern	Dapol	2017
Class 319	Midland/Southern	Bachmann	TBA
Class 321	Midland/Eastern	Revolution Trains	TBA
Class 390	Midland	Revolution Trains	2017

Hatton's new 'OO' gauge '14XX' 0-4-2T is expected to arrive before the end of 2016.

Golden Valley Hobbies' 'Janus' 0-6-0 diesel shunter is being developed by Oxford Rail for release in 2017.

The 'N' gauge Class 40 will feature a Next18 decoder socket, provision for installation of sound and directional lighting too.

Bachmann's LNWR 'Coal Tank' for 'OO' broke cover in late August.

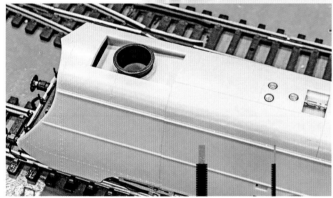

The Hornby air-smoothed 'Merchant Navy' is to be released in the first quarter of 2017.

Minerva Model Railways' second 'O' gauge locomotive is the Kerr Stuart 'Victory' 0-6-0T.

Heljan's next 'O' gauge diesel release will be the Class 37/0 with centre headcodes.

The Little Loco Company's debut locomotive is the BTH Class 15 for 'O' gauge. Development has been swift.

The Stanier 'Mogul' will be the next big steam release from Bachmann for 'OO'.

Next in for 'N' gauge from Bachmann's Graham Farish brand is the all new GWR 'Castle' 4-6-0 which will feature a Next18 decoder socket and factory sound in one version too.

with the 'Large Prairie' due for release first during 2017.

More new ground has been broken for the scale too with Hatton's of Liverpool announcing in August that it is working with Heljan to produce both the 'A3' and 'A4' LNER 'Pacifics' as well as a range of ready-to-run Gresley teak corridor stock for 'O' gauge as exclusive commissions too.

Minerva Models has announced two further locomotives during the past 12 months in the Kerr Stuart 'Victory' 0-6-0T and the GWR '57XX' 0-6-0PT. The latter is in direct competition with announcement of the same locomotive class by Dapol following its merger with Lionheart Trains.

Redressing the balance, Dapol also announced it would be producing the Fowler 'Jinty' 0-6-0T in 2017 too as its fourth 'O' gauge locomotive.

A new name in diesel locomotives for the scale appeared in spring 2016 when the Little Loco Company revealed its plan to produce the British Thompson Houston Class 15 Bo-Bo. This high specification model - which includes built in speakers, a Plux22 decoder socket and controllable lighting - is expected to become available before the end of 2016, offering a new choice of manufacturer for the scale.

Table 3 details the full list of ready-to-run mass-produced 'O' gauge locomotives currently planned.

Overview

While 2016 has definitely seen a slower rate of new announcements, the number of new locomotive projects planned as ready-to-run models is now at its highest level in four years with 87 on the list – that's up eight from 2015 and even up by five on 2014 when 82 models were in the throes of development.

'O' gauge has seen a massive growth in manufacturer interest during 2016 and we expect to see more of the same in 2017 – especially as the list is delivered. 'N' gauge and 'OO' gauge are stable while the commission and crowd-funded portion of the market remain buoyant for niche models which otherwise wouldn't be produced.

Oxford Rail's second locomotive – the GWR 'Dean Goods' 0-6-0 – is due to arrive in the shops before the end of 2016.

TABLE 3 - 'O' GAUGE NEW RELEASES FOR 2016-2017			
Class	**Region**	**Manufacturer**	**Expected**
GWR '43XX' 2-6-0	Western	Heljan	2017
GWR '57XX' 0-6-0PT	Western	Dapol	TBA
GWR '57XX' 0-6-0PT	Western	Minerva Model Railways	2017
GWR '61XX' 2-6-2T	Western	Heljan	2016
LMS 'Jinty' 0-6-0T	Midland	Dapol	2017
LNER 'A3' 4-6-2	Eastern	Hatton's/Heljan	2018
LNER 'A4' 4-6-2	Eastern	Hatton's/Heljan	2018
Hunslet 'J94' 0-6-0ST	Eastern	DJ Models	TBA
Kerr Stuart 'Victory' 0-6-0T	Industrial	Minerva Model Railways	2016
Class 03	Various	Heljan	TBA
Class 05	Midland/Eastern	Heljan	2017
Class 08	Various	Dapol	2016
Class 15	Eastern	Little Loco Company	2016
Class 23	Eastern	DJ Models	TBA
Class 37 (centre headcode)	Various	Heljan	2017
Class 45	Midland	Heljan	2017
Class 117	Western/Midland	Heljan	TBA
Class 120	Western	Heljan	TBA
Class 121	Western/Midland	Heljan	TBA
Class 128	Western/Midland	Heljan	2017

The phrase 'we have never had it so good' has been used time and time again over the past decade, but it is true. Moreover, manufacturers are beginning to look more closely at the technology which can be installed in models as users begin to demand more operational value from the products. SLW's Class 24 showed that potential superbly, while during demonstrations on *Hornby Magazine's* layout, the 'N' gauge sound-fitted Class 108 from Bachmann has drawn significant attention. The arrival of Dapol's Black Label Gresley 'A4' 4-6-2 will be one to watch closely too as it offers a specification which has never been seen before in mainstream ready-to-run with built in smoke generator, sound and a DCC decoder in all models.

We hope the technology trend will continue and spread throughout all parts of model manufacture so that we see better models not just on the outside, but on the inside too. ∎

THE HEADLINES			
Planned 'OO' gauge new releases			
	2013	2014	2015	2016
Steam:	17	26	25	21
Diesel:	13	18	20	25
Total:	30	44	45	46
Planned 'N' gauge new releases			
	2013	2014	2015	2016
Steam:	15	17	13	9
Diesel:	15	11	12	14
Total:	30	28	25	23
Planned 'O' gauge new releases			
	2013	2014	2015	2016
Steam:	3	3	3	9
Diesel:	9	9	7	11
Total:	12	12	10	20
Overall total:	72	82	79	87

Hornby's Peckett 'W4' 0-4-0ST is a tiny model – and due for release in November 2016.